THE ULTIMATE COCKTAIL BOOK

THE PYRAMID APPROACH
TO STOCKING YOUR DRINKS CUPBOARD

THE
ULTIMATE
COCKTAIL BOOK
THE PYRAMID APPROACH
TO STOCKING YOUR DRINKS CUPBOARD

M. C. Martin

JOHN
WAITE

This book is based on an idea by Gwyn Headley and
Yvonne Seeley, with grateful thanks

Published by John Waite Ltd 1983
14 Hartington Villas, Hove, Sussex, England

© 1983, John Waite Ltd

ISBN 0 946714 00 2

Printed and bound in Great Britain by
Biddles of Guildford

Illustrations by John Bradbury
Cover photography by Julian Moss
Typeset by Interimprint, Brighton

CONTENTS

PREFACE

There has never before been a cocktail book as practical and as **useful** as THE ULTIMATE COCKTAIL BOOK. No more that frustrating hunt for a cocktail for which you have **all** the ingredients because with this book, arranged in 43 logical and progressive sections, you simply open the page at the level which your cocktail cabinet has reached and you should be able to mix all the drinks included in the book up to then.

The Pyramid Approach to stocking your drinks cupboard is a simple and sensible system which keeps one eye on pleasure and the other on your pocket. You move progressively from cocktails which can be made from just a bottle of gin, Angostura bitters and the contents of any decent larder, adding, when finances and foreign holidays permit, a bottle at a time until you have the range to undertake even the most exotic concoctions.

This means you can start right in mixing, getting the taste buds excited, with only the most limited store of bottles.

And by the time your cupboard contains all the bottles listed in the CONTENTS, your cocktail repertoire will have reached **over 600** sociable and exquisitely delicious reasons for having a cocktail!

And if you're starting off with a cupboard not quite bare, there is an alphabetical INDEX to help you to find the drink you're looking for instantly.

But all the time you're adding bottles you'll be able to tempt your palate with a blossoming range of 'the cocktail that cheers'. The *Pyramid Approach* is really the only way sensibly and practically to arrange a cocktail book.

INTRODUCTION

There's a saying that if you know what a person is going to drink, you know all there is to know about him. And none of us wants to be as predictable as that. There's another saying (it's Compton MacKenzie's) that some of us are born two drinks under par.

Well, this book is designed for interesting people who can be even more interesting after they have imbibed a couple (or so) of cocktails.

You don't need much in the way of equipment to become a cocktail drinker and you'll probably stay one for ever: a pair of bottles (and arguably the least expensive way to start is with a bottle of gin and one of Angostura bitters), some ice and a glass. If you can manage to have in stock a selection of fresh fruit juices, a bottle of grenadine (also cheap) and that magical and beautiful gadget, a cocktail shaker, then you're well away.

To obtain fullest value from this abundance of recipes, it's a good idea to have some notion of the background to cocktails and why they are so good, and also to know a little about methods and equipment and those little touches which turn a pretty and sophisticated drink into something special.

Mixed drinks, possets or cups, negus, mulled wines or ales and grog have been known for some hundreds of years but the first modern cocktail to make its way into print was described in 1806 and by the later 1800s several cocktail books had been published. But it is only since the 1920s and '30s that in the USA and in Britain cocktails, as we know them now, have become so popular. The popularity of cocktail drinking is the UK then faded somewhat but a great resurgence of interest has taken place over the last decade, and, with this renewal of interest, has grown an even more extensive range of spirits, liqueurs, aperitifs and cordials with which the discriminating drinker may experiment.

Of the seven thousand or so cocktails which it is claimed have been invented, naturally some are rather less than wonderful but many are works of genius in their sheer simplicity (the greatest of all

INTRODUCTION

is, of course, the DRY MARTINI — 6 or 7 parts gin to one of dry vermouth), in their æsthetic beauty or in the originality of the taste of
the blended flavours. Some cocktails have stood the test of time;
they are for regular drinking. Others are for special occasions or for
when nothing will do but to have a BOOSTER (brandy, Cointreau
and the white of an egg, with nutmeg sprinkled on top). After all,
meat, bread and potatoes are eaten all the time but smoked salmon
and asparagus do not feature very often in our everyday menus.
Again, as in books on haute cuisine, there is always a cocktail which
is fun to read about even if the reader feels that it is unlikely ever to
make its way into his or her own particular shaker. At least the
imagination can be titillated!

There are basic principles attached to a cocktail. It needs a **base**, a
spirit, wine or liqueur, *a modifier*, to smooth the mixture — wine, fruit
juices, sugar, eggs or cream and a special *flavouring or colouring*
of a fruit syrup, a liqueur or a cordial. Not all cocktails contain all
three and there are occasions when the juxtaposition of two distinct
base spirits does work. Gin and rum can go well together for
example. But bearing this theory in mind can prevent the experi-
menter from inventing a fairly unappetizing concoction — something
easy to do when one is trying to find some use for the last half-inch
remaining in several very different bottles. This is not to say 'never
experiment' of course. None of these recipes would have existed at
all unless someone had applied imagination and trial and error too,
no doubt.

But bearing the theory in mind will perhaps enable the mixer to
come up with a new cocktail which becomes a classic — or failing
that, at least a subject of much personal satisfaction over the years!

Methods
There are three basic ways of making a cocktail — shaking, stirring
and, less frequently, blending. On all occasions the cocktail must be
served cold and this means having a good supply of ice available,
for the cocktail itself or for chilling the glasses and equipment.

To shake a cocktail you need a cocktail shaker. It doesn't matter,
as far as the taste is concerned, in which order the ingredients are
put into the shaker, but it is sensible to put in the ice first (so that the
liquids have longer to chill) and then the other contents roughly in
order of cost, so that, should something go wrong half-way
through, your loss is minimized. Either shaved or cracked ice can

A The classic cocktail glass. Contains about 6 fl oz. The stem may be coloured or decorated but the bowl should always be clear to display the beauty of the contents. **B** The Old Fashioned or Rocks glass. For Whisky or any drink served on the rocks. Chunky always, but varieties of size and shape, often crystal. Contains 6-8 fl oz. **C/D** Highball and Collins tumblers. Contain 8-12 fl oz, depending on height. Either straight-sided or slightly flaring, they are used for all long drinks, including beer. **E** An attractive, but not strictly essential glass, for serving Sours and Fizzes. Contains about 6 fl oz. **F** The Ballon or balloon glass. Large and with inward sloping sides to retain the aroma of brandy, but is also useful for beer (half a pint) or long drinks which need ice in the bottom of the glass. Contains about 10 fl oz. **G** Sherry glass. To contain only 2-3 fl oz, so that the sherry does not become too warm while you are drinking. **H** A liqueur glass, containing only 1-2 fl oz. Often crystal or with an etched design to display the rich colours of liqueurs to the full. **I** A Pousse-café glass. Taller than a liqueur glass and with parallel sides to show off the stripes of the drink. **J** Goblets come in a number of sizes and shapes and are used for red and white wine and often for cocktails too. **K** The Champagne Tulip and the Champagne Saucer. Somehow the Saucer is more festive but the Tulip does hold the effervescence for longer. **L** For hot punches and toddies, a tumbler with surrounding handle prevents blistering of the hand!

INTRODUCTION

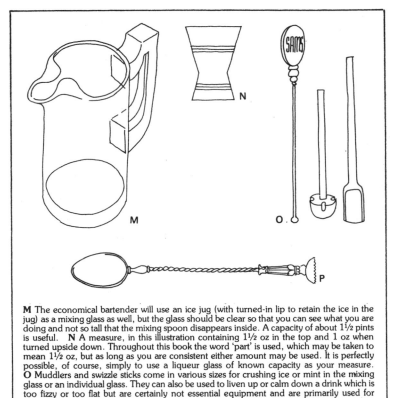

M The economical bartender will use an ice jug (with turned-in lip to retain the ice in the jug) as a mixing glass as well, but the glass should be clear so that you can see what you are doing and not so tall that the mixing spoon disappears inside. A capacity of about 1½ pints is useful. **N** A measure, in this illustration containing 1½ oz in the top and 1 oz when turned upside down. Throughout this book the word 'part' is used, which may be taken to mean 1½ oz, but as long as you are consistent either amount may be used. It is perfectly possible, of course, simply to use a liqueur glass of known capacity as your measure. **O** Muddlers and swizzle sticks come in various sizes for crushing ice or mint in the mixing glass or an individual glass. They can also be used to liven up or calm down a drink which is too fizzy or too flat but are certainly not essential equipment and are primarily used for decoration or for fun. **P** A Bar spoon or mixing spoon. Handle about 10in long, often spiral to provide grip. The non-business end is often designed to be used as a muddler.

be used or, usually simpler to lay hands on, cubed ice. Shake vigorously, keeping a hand and finger round the upper parts of the shaker to prevent them scattering. The cocktail – and your hands! – chill very quickly. If you shake long enough for the rattle of the ice inside to quieten down you have probably diluted the drink too much. Judge the compromise moment to pour.

Stirring or mixing is usually done in a clear glass jug, pint-sized or slightly larger is fine, with a lip for pouring. Stir with a long mixing spoon, again not for too long or the ice will dilute the drink too much, but just until beads of condensation appear on the jug. Using this method the drink remains clear, rather than becoming cloudy as it does in a shaker.

When using eggs or fresh fruit in a cocktail, an electric blender is recommended. Do use cracked, rather than cube, ice to reduce the chances of damage to the blender and do not put fizzy liquids in until after you have blended. Using a blender, the cocktail will be smooth and fluffy.

All the recipes in this book specify which method to use.

Muddling is a simple trick used when making, for example, an Old Fashioned or a Julep. It is simply the poking and crushing of a sugar cube or sprig of mint with a spoon until dissolved or the juice has been squeezed out.

Sometimes a cocktail is made using none of these methods but

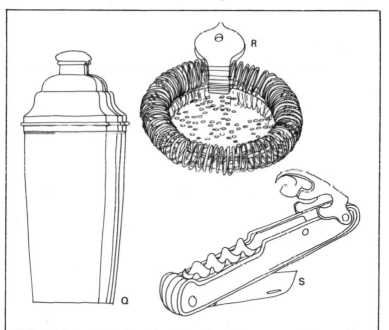

Q Cocktail shaker. Usually in stainless steel or silver, in three sections; the largest, lower section to contain the ice and liquids, the upper part, with integral strainer, for pouring the cocktail after the cap has been removed. Always keep a finger or two on the cap when shaking! R A Hawthorne strainer. Should be made of stainless steel. Prevents ice from the mixing glass falling into the cocktail. S A 'bartender's friend' – an extremely handy device for opening all kinds of bottles and cans.

INTRODUCTION

just by relying on the different specific gravities of the liquids involved. In this case, one pours the heaviest into the glass first and the others in decreasing order of density, either very gently down the side of a straight-sided glass or over the back of a teaspoon, to achieve a very attractive layered effect. There are a number of recipes for a POUSSE-CAFÉ, all slightly over the top – the Traffic Light, for example; Green Crème de Menthe, Yellow Chartreuse, Maraschino. Then stop.

Equipment
Some of the more essential equipment is illustrated in the previous pages but a number of other items will be found to be extremely useful also. For the ice you need an **ice bucket**, preferably some **ice tongs** too. A **wooden chopping block** and a **sharp knife** will be needed for cutting and preparing fruit and a **lemon squeezer** is handy for the extraction of those fresh fruit juices. You should have a **drying cloth** to polish glasses and a **wet cloth** to wipe up the almost inevitable occasional spillages and to keep your cocktail area spotlessly clean. The well-heeled cocktail drinker will be keen to buy an **ice crusher** but an effective, if noisy, substitute is to wrap cubes of ice in a tea-towel and beat them into submission with a rolling-pin.

Non-alcoholic matters
The contents of your larder must be considered. Used much in cocktails are fresh fruit juices and it is advisable to have on hand orange, lemon, pineapple and grapefruit. Angostura bitters, Worcestershire sauce and Tabasco, together with grated nutmeg, are also important and are generally to be found in all good food cupboards.

Syrups are inexpensive and the two most useful will be found to be Grenadine and Orgeat, the former made from pomegranates, the latter, almond based. Sugar syrup may also be purchased though it is perfectly easy to make yourself by bringing slowly to the boil a pint of water and a pound of sugar.

And of course there are **garnishes** – olives, cocktail onions, cherries, mint, slices of lemon or orange, with or without cocktail sticks, and those pretty little paper parasols.

With these preparations made and with a bottle or two in hand it is hoped that you will have an extremely pleasant period of many years with the more than 600 recipes contained in the rest of this book.

GIN 40%   A form of gin dates back to the mid-sixteenth century; it was a spirit distilled from rye and flavoured with juniper and was used for medicinal purposes. Dry gin, as we know it today, is a grain distillate redistilled with juniper berries and flavoured with coriander, angelica root, cinnamon and cassia bark, orange and lemon peel and almonds.

London Dry is the gin selected as the base spirit of many of the following cocktails. Plymouth Gin is slightly sweeter, and Holland Gin is highly flavoured and aromatic; it is a form of schnapps and is rarely used in cocktails.

ACE

3 parts gin
1 part grenadine
1 part cream
½ egg white
5 drops lemon juice
nutmeg to taste

Shake vigorously and strain into a medium-sized glass. Sprinkle a little nutmeg on top and serve.

ASTOR

1 generous measure of dry gin
1 dash lemon juice
1 dash orange juice

Stir well and strain into a cocktail glass. Twist orange and lemon peel over and serve.

BEBBO

2 parts dry gin
1 part lemon juice
½ tsp orange juice
½ tsp honey

Shake vigorously and strain into a cocktail glass.

BELMONT

2 parts gin
1 part grenadine
1 tsp cream

Shake well and strain into a cocktail glass.

BENNETT

3 parts dry gin
1 part lime juice
2 dashes Angostura bitters

Shake well and strain into a cocktail glass. Half a teaspoon of sugar may be added if wished.

CLOVER CLUB

2 parts dry gin
1 part grenadine
juice of ½ lemon or 1 lime
1 egg white

GIN

Shake well and strain into a medium-sized glass. If this cocktail is served with a sprig of mint on top it is called a CLOVER LEAF.

DF

1 part gin
1 part grapefruit juice
½ tsp grenadine

Stir well and strain into a cocktail glass.

FROTH BLOWER

1 generous measure of gin
4 dashes grenadine
1 egg white

Shake well and strain into a wine-glass.

GIMLET

1 part gin
1 part lime juice cordial
  (preferably Rose's)

Stir well in a whisky tumbler and add ice.

GIN COCKTAIL

1 generous measure of gin
4 dashes orange bitters

Shake well and strain into a cocktail glass. This is also called a WAX COCKTAIL.

GIN FIZZ

1 generous measure of gin
juice of ½ lemon
½ tbsp sugar

This is very similar to a TOM COLLINS but shorter. It should be well shaken, strained into a medium-sized glass and topped up with soda water, preferably from a syphon.

GIN SLING

1 generous measure of gin
1 tsp sugar
1 dash Angostura bitters
  (optional)

Dissolve 1 teaspoon of sugar in a little water in a tall glass, add the gin and top up with water or soda water. Add a lump of ice if served cold; if served hot, grate a little nutmeg on top.

GIN SOUR

1 generous measure of dry gin
juice of ½ lemon
1 tsp sugar
1 dash orange bitters (optional)

Shake well and strain into a medium-sized glass. Add a little soda. Serve with a slice of orange and a cherry. Brandy, whisky, bourbon and other sours can all be made to the same recipe.

HARROVIAN

1 generous measure of dry gin
1 tsp orange juice
1 dash Angostura bitters
1 dash lemon juice

Shake well and strain into a cock-tail glass.

HONOLULU

1 generous measure of dry gin
1 dash Angostura bitters
1 dash lemon juice
1 dash orange juice
1 dash pineapple juice
1/4 tsp sugar

Shake well and strain into a cocktail glass.

MAGNOLIA BLOSSOM

2 parts gin
1 part lemon juice
1 part cream
1 dash grenadine

Shake well and strain into a cocktail glass.

MR MANHATTAN

1 generous measure of gin
1 dash lemon juice
4 dashes orange juice
1 sugar lump
4 fresh mint leaves

Crush sugar lump in shaker, crush mint leaves and add with the rest of the ingredients. Shake well and strain into a cocktail glass.

NEW ORLEANS FIZZ

4 parts gin
2 parts lemon juice
2 parts lime juice
2 parts sugar syrup
1 part cream
1 egg white

Shake well and strain into a tall glass. Add a little soda, but this drink should be served quite thick.

ORANGE BLOSSOM I

1 part dry gin
1 part orange juice

Shake well and strain into a cocktail glass. Serve with a slice of orange.

PINK GIN

1 generous measure of gin
1 dash Angostura bitters

Shake the bitters into a wineglass and roll them around to coat the inside surface. Then shake out any surplus, add the gin and a lump of ice if wished. This cocktail is usually made with Plymouth gin, which is slightly sweeter, in keeping with its naval tradition.

PINK LADY

2 parts gin
1 part grenadine
1 egg white
1 part cream (optional)
1 dash lime juice (optional)

Shake well and strain into a medium-sized glass. Some recipes call for the addition of cream and lime juice.

ROYAL CLOVER CLUB

1 generous measure of gin
juice of 1/2 lemon
1 tbsp grenadine
1 egg yolk

Shake well and strain into a medium-sized glass.

GIN

SILVER KING

*1 generous measure of gin
juice of ¼ lemon
1 tsp sugar
2 dashes orange bitters
1 egg white*

Shake well and strain into a medium-sized glass.

TOM COLLINS

*1 generous measure of dry gin
juice of ½ lemon
½ tbsp sugar*

Shake well until sugar has dissolved, strain into a tall glass and add ice and soda to top up. The addition of sprigs of fresh mint make this a SOUTH SIDE. A JOHN COLLINS is made by substituting bourbon for the gin.

WEST INDIAN

*1 generous measure of dry gin
1 tsp lemon juice
1 tsp sugar
4 dashes Angostura bitters*

Stir with one lump of ice in a cocktail glass. Squeeze lemon peel over drink, and decorate with a slice of lemon.

WHITE ROSE

*4 parts gin
1 part lemon juice
2 parts orange juice
1 egg white
1 tsp sugar (optional)*

Shake well and strain into a medium-sized glass. Serve with a cherry, a slice of lemon and a slice of orange.

DRY VERMOUTH

DRY VERMOUTH 18%   Vermouth was first produced commercially in the late eighteenth century. By the 1880s the House of Cinzano was flourishing and vermouth was enjoyed internationally. Sweet vermouth came to be known as 'Italian' and dry vermouth as 'French' but there is no longer any geographical justification for this. Vermouths are fortified wines infused with numerous herbs and spices and made according to extremely complex and closely-guarded recipes. A chief ingredient of dry vermouth is camomile, but all brands differ. Try out several until you find the one you like.

ASTORIA

1 part dry vermouth
2 parts gin
1 dash orange bitters

Stir well and strain into a well-chilled cocktail glass. Serve with a stuffed olive.

ATTA BOY

1 part dry vermouth
2 parts dry gin
4 dashes grenadine

Shake well and strain into a cocktail glass.

BLINTON

1 part dry vermouth
1 part gin
1 dash Angostura bitters

Stir well and strain into a cocktail glass. Add a second dash of Angostura bitters, serve with an olive and you have a GOLF

BRONX TERRACE

1 part dry vermouth
2 parts gin
juice of ½ lime

Shake well and strain into a cocktail glass.

DRY MARTINI

1 part dry vermouth
6 parts dry gin

Put several ice cubes into a mixing glass, add the gin and vermouth and stir quickly but well. Then, before the ice can melt, strain the liquid into a chilled cocktail glass. A twist of lemon or an olive may be added if wished, although both give a touch of oiliness to the drink. Some Martini lovers prefer to add their lemon by squeezing a sliver of rind, skinside down, over the glass. The proportions of gin to dry vermouth in a Martini are argued about endlessly. Experiment until you find the drink to suit you, from 3:1 to 15:1.

DRY VERMOUTH

GENE TUNNEY

1 part dry vermouth
2 parts gin
1 dash lemon juice
1 dash orange juice

Shake well and strain into a cocktail glass.

GIBSON

1 part dry vermouth
6 parts dry gin
1 pearl onion

This is made in the same way as a DRY MARTINI, substituting a pearl onion for the olive.

IDEAL

1 part dry vermouth
2 parts dry gin
1 part grapefruit juice
1 tsp sugar
2 or 3 dashes orange or
   Angostura bitters

Shake until sugar dissolves and strain into a cocktail glass.

JACK PINE

1 part dry vermouth
2 parts dry gin
1 part orange juice
1 slice pineapple

Shake vigorously and strain into a cocktail glass.

THREE STRIPES

1 part dry vermouth
2 parts gin
3 slices orange

Shake vigorously and strain into a cocktail glass.

ZANZIBAR

6 parts dry vermouth
2 parts gin
1 part lemon juice
1 part sugar syrup
1 dash orange bitters (optional)

Shake well and strain into a cocktail glass. Serve with a twist of lemon.

SWEET VERMOUTH

SWEET VERMOUTH 16%   This is also known as Italian vermouth, although it is made in other countries, especially France. A chief ingredient of sweet vermouth is vanilla, but there are many other herbs and spices in its complex recipe, including iris root, quinine, Chinese rhubarb, and various citrus peels.

ADDINGTON

1 part sweet vermouth
1 part dry vermouth

Stir well and strain into a medium-sized glass. Top up with soda and squeeze orange peel over.

APPLE PIE I

2 parts sweet vermouth
6 parts apple juice
1 part lime juice

Shake well and strain into a tall glass. Top up with soda water and serve with a slice of apple and lemon.

BOSTONIAN

1 part sweet vermouth
4 parts gin
½ tsp lemon juice
½ tsp orange juice
½ tsp sugar syrup
3 sprigs fresh mint

Crush the mint with the fruit juices, add the rest of the ingredients, shake well and strain into a medium-sized glass. This may be served with a slice of lemon and orange and a sprig of fresh mint.

BROADWAY SPECIAL

1 part sweet vermouth
2 parts gin
2 dashes grenadine
½ tsp pineapple juice
½ egg white
nutmeg to taste

Shake vigorously and strain into a medium-sized glass. Sprinkle nutmeg over and serve.

BRONX

1 part sweet vermouth
3 parts dry gin
1 part dry vermouth
1 part orange juice

Shake well and strain into a cocktail glass. Cut the gin to one part and you have a YELLOW RATTLER.

BRONX SILVER

1 part sweet vermouth
2 parts dry gin
1 part dry vermouth
juice of ¼ orange
1 egg white

Shake well and strain into a wineglass.

SWEET VERMOUTH

CRYSTAL BRONX

1 part sweet vermouth
1 part dry vermouth
1 part orange juice

Pour over a lump of ice into a tall glass and top with soda. This is sometimes called a WYOMING SWING, when it should be served with a slice of orange.

FIBBER McGEE

1 part sweet vermouth
3 parts dry gin
1 part grapefruit juice
2 dashes Angostura bitters

Stir well and strain into a cocktail glass. Serve with a twist of lemon.

GIN and IT

1 part sweet vermouth
2 parts gin

Pour over an ice cube into a cocktail glass, stir well and serve with a cherry. The 'It' is short for Italian, sweet vermouth being described as 'Italian' and dry as 'French'. This is sometimes known as a SWEET MARTINI.

HOMESTEAD

1 part sweet vermouth
2 parts dry gin
1 slice of orange

Shake vigorously and strain into a cocktail glass. If you reverse the quantities of gin and vermouth it is called a VELOCITY.

INCOME TAX

1 part sweet vermouth
2 parts dry gin
1 part dry vermouth
juice of ¼ orange
1 dash Angostura bitters

Shake well and strain into a cocktail glass.

MEDIUM MARTINI

1 part sweet vermouth
2 parts gin
1 part dry vermouth

Pour over ice into a cocktail glass, stir well and serve with a twist of lemon peel.

MILLIONAIRE I

1 part sweet vermouth
2 parts gin
1 tbsp pineapple juice
1 tsp grenadine
1 egg white

Shake well and strain into a medium-sized glass. This is sometimes called a MILLION DOLLAR cocktail.

PERFECT

1 part sweet vermouth
1 part dry gin
1 part dry vermouth

Shake well and strain into a cocktail glass. The addition of a sprig of mint turns this into a COOPERSTOWN COCKTAIL. Substitute 2 dashes of orange bitters for the mint and you have a LONE TREE, or a dash of fresh orange juice instead of the bitters makes ONE EXCITING NIGHT.

PLAZA

1 part sweet vermouth
1 part dry gin
1 part dry vermouth
1 slice pineapple

Shake vigorously and strain into a cocktail glass. Serve with a slice of pineapple.

POLO

1 part sweet vermouth
1 part dry gin
1 part dry vermouth
juice of ¼ lemon or ½ lime

Shake well and strain into a cocktail glass. Double the quantity of gin and use pineapple juice instead of the lime or lemon and you have a QUEEN'S COCKTAIL.

RAYMOND

1 generous measure of sweet
  vermouth
1 slice pineapple
1 tbsp orange juice
1 dash orange bitters

Shake well and strain into a cocktail glass. Serve with a slice of orange.

SMILER

1 part sweet vermouth
2 parts dry gin
1 part dry vermouth
1 dash Angostura bitters
1 dash orange bitters

Shake well and strain into a cocktail glass.

TROCADERO

1 part sweet vermouth
1 part dry vermouth
1 dash orange bitters
1 dash grenadine

Stir well and strain into a cocktail glass. Squeeze lemon peel over the glass and serve with a cherry.

TWIN SIX

1 part sweet vermouth
2 parts dry gin
1 dash grenadine
3 slices orange
1 egg white

Shake vigorously and strain into a medium-sized glass.

VERMOUTH COCKTAIL

1 generous measure of sweet or
  dry vermouth
1 dash Angostura bitters or
  4 dashes orange bitters

Stir well and strain into a cocktail glass.

SHERRY

SHERRY 15-18%   At its best sherry is made from white grapes grown in the Jerez region of Spain, fermented, fortified with brandy and then matured. Dry sherry (fino) is pale and light, medium (amontillado) is richer, sweeter and slightly darker, and sweet sherry (oloroso) is dark, full-bodied and rich; it is made by adding a very sweet, dark liqueur wine to the fino.

ADONIS

2 parts dry sherry
1 part sweet vermouth
1 dash Angostura or orange
  bitters

Stir well and strain into a cocktail glass. Squeeze orange peel over.

BAMBOO

2 parts dry sherry
1 part dry vermouth
2 dashes orange bitters
2 drops Angostura bitters

Stir well and strain into a cocktail glass. Serve with a green olive.

CUPID

1 generous measure of sherry
1 egg
1 tsp sugar
pinch of Cayenne pepper

Shake well and strain into a medium-sized glass.

DUKE OF MARLBOROUGH

1 part sherry
1 part sweet vermouth
3 dashes orange bitters

Stir well and strain into a cocktail glass. Squeeze orange peel over.

INCA

1 part dry sherry
1 part dry vermouth
1 part gin
1 part sweet vermouth
1 dash orange or Angostura
  bitters
1 dash orgeat syrup

Stir well and strain into a cocktail glass. Orgeat is an almond-flavoured non-alcoholic syrup.

JEREZ COCKTAIL

1 generous measure of sherry
1 dash orange bitters
1 dash peach bitters

Stir well and strain into a cocktail glass. Peach bitters are sometimes hard to obtain, but this is worth making if you can get hold of a bottle.

REFORM

2 parts sherry
1 part dry vermouth
1 dash orange bitters

Stir well, strain into a cocktail glass and serve with a cherry.

SHERRY COBBLER

1 generous measure of sherry
1 tsp sugar
1 dash grenadine

Pour into a tall glass, stir in sugar and grenadine, add cracked ice, top up with soda water and stir.

SHERRY COCKTAIL

1 generous measure of sherry
4 dashes dry vermouth
4 dashes orange bitters

Stir well and strain into a cocktail glass.

SHERRY & EGG

1 generous measure of sherry
1 egg

Carefully crack an egg into a wineglass. Pour the sherry on top and serve.

SHERRY FLIP

1 generous measure of dry sherry
1 egg
1 tsp sugar
2 dashes Angostura bitters

Shake briskly and strain into a medium-sized glass. Serve with a pinch of nutmeg.

SHERRY SANGAREE

1 generous measure of sherry
1 tsp sugar syrup

Mix in a small tumbler. Fill with shaved ice and serve with a dusting of nutmeg.

UTILITY

2 parts sherry
1 part dry vermouth
1 part sweet vermouth

Stir well and strain into a cocktail glass.

DUBONNET

DUBONNET 17% A popular French aperitif made from red wine, Dubonnet has a pronounced quinine flavour.

APPETIZER

1 part Dubonnet
1 part gin
juice of ½ orange

Shake well and strain into a cocktail glass.

AVIATOR

1 part Dubonnet
1 part dry gin
1 part dry vermouth
1 part sweet vermouth

Stir well and strain into a cocktail glass.

CORONATION

1 part Dubonnet
1 part dry gin
1 part dry vermouth

Stir well and strain into a cocktail glass. This is sometimes called a SALOME.

DIABOLA

2 parts Dubonnet
1 part gin
2 dashes orgeat syrup

Shake well and strain into a cocktail glass.

DUBONNET COCKTAIL

1 part Dubonnet
1 part dry gin

Stir well and strain into a cocktail glass. A DUBONNET DRY can be made by using a ratio of 2:1 gin to Dubonnet and serving it with a twist of lemon peel. Another variation includes rinsing out the cocktail glass with dry vermouth.

SOUL KISS I

1 part Dubonnet
2 parts dry vermouth
2 parts sweet vermouth
1 part orange juice

Shake well and strain into a cocktail glass.

UPSTAIRS

1 generous measure Dubonnet
juice of ¼ lemon

Pour into a medium-sized glass, add cracked ice and top up with soda. This is otherwise known as a DUBONNET HIGHBALL.

LIGHT RUM

LIGHT RUM 40-75% Rum is a distillation of molasses and is produced in most of the countries where sugar cane is grown. All rums vary but they tend to fall into one of three categories: light-bodied and pale such as Cuban or Puerto Rican rums; rich, full-bodied, strong-flavoured, dark rums such as Jamaican; and aromatic rums like the Demeraras. There are many varieties available so it is best to experiment until you find the one you like. Although, for light rum certainly, a bottle of Bacardi will prove very useful as a not too overpowering base.

BACARDI BLOSSOM

3 parts Bacardi
1 part orange juice
1/2 tsp lemon juice
1/2 tsp sugar

Shake well and strain into a cocktail glass. Serve with a dusting of nutmeg.

BACARDI COCKTAIL

1 measure Bacardi
juice of 1/2 lime
1/2 tsp sugar

Shake well and strain into a cocktail glass. If you substitute a half measure of grenadine for the sugar this is called a BLOOD TRANSFUSION.

BACARDI DRY

1 part Bacardi
1 part dry vermouth

Stir well and strain into a cocktail glass.

BACARDI DUBONNET

1 part Bacardi
1 part Dubonnet
1/2 tsp grenadine
1/2 tsp lime juice

Stir well and strain into a cocktail glass.

BACARDI SILVER

1 part Bacardi
1 part dry gin
1 part pineapple juice
1/2 tsp lemon juice
1/2 egg white

Shake well and strain into a medium-sized glass. Serve with a cherry.

BACARDI SPECIAL

2 parts Bacardi
1 part dry gin
1 tsp grenadine
juice of 1/2 lime

Shake well and strain into a cocktail glass.

LIGHT RUM

BACARDI SWEET

1 part Bacardi
1 part sweet vermouth

Stir well and strain into a cocktail glass. This is also called a LITTLE PRINCESS or a POKER.

BERRY

4 parts rum
1 part orange juice
1 part pineapple juice
1 dash grenadine

Shake well and strain into a cocktail glass.

BLUE BOY

3 parts light rum
1 part sweet vermouth
1/2 tsp orange juice
1 dash Angostura bitters

Shake well and strain. Substitute lemon for the orange and you have a ZAMBA.

BOLO

1 measure Bacardi
juice of 1/4 lemon or 1/2 lime
juice of 1/4 orange
1 tsp sugar

Shake well and strain into a cocktail glass.

BUMPER

6 parts light rum
1 part gin
1 dash lemon juice

Stir well and strain into a cocktail glass. Twist lemon peel over the glass.

BVD

1 part Bacardi
1 part dry vermouth
1 part Dubonnet

Stir well and strain into a cocktail glass. Gin is sometimes used instead of Dubonnet.

CARIBBEAN CREOLE

2 parts light rum
1 part lime juice
1 part cream
2 dashes grenadine

Shake well and strain into a medium-sized glass filled with crushed ice. It looks pretty when served with a sprig of fresh mint, and should be drunk through straws.

CHAPARRA

1 part light rum
1 part sweet vermouth
1/2 tsp sugar

Shake well, strain into a cocktail glass and serve with a spiral of lemon peel.

CUBA LIBRE

1 part light rum
1 part Coca Cola
juice of 1/2 lime

Shake well and strain into a medium-sized glass.

CUBAN COCKTAIL I

2 parts Bacardi
1 part lemon juice
1 tsp sugar

Shake well and strain into a cocktail glass.

DAIQUIRI

2 parts Bacardi
1 part fresh lime juice
1 tsp sugar

Shake well and strain into a well-chilled cocktail glass.

DAVIS

2 parts rum
1 part dry vermouth
2 dashes grenadine
juice of ½ lemon or 1 lime

Shake well and strain into a cocktail glass.

DUNLOP

2 parts rum
1 part sherry
1 dash Angostura bitters

Stir well and strain into a cocktail glass.

FIG LEAF

1 part rum
2 parts dry vermouth
juice of ½ lime
dash of Angostura bitters

Shake well and strain into a cocktail glass.

FLORIDA SPECIAL

3 parts rum
1 part grapefruit juice
1 tsp dry vermouth
1 tsp sweet vermouth

Shake well and strain into a medium-sized glass.

FORT LAUDERDALE

4 parts light rum
2 parts sweet vermouth
1 part lime juice
1 part orange juice

Shake well and strain into a medium-sized glass. Serve with a slice of orange and a cherry.

HAVANA BEACH

1 part light rum
2 parts pineapple juice
1 tsp sugar
½ fresh lime
ginger ale to top up

Chop lime into four pieces and put them with the other ingredients into a shaker or, even better, into a blender. Shake vigorously, pour into a tall glass and top up with ginger ale. Serve with a slice of lime and a cherry.

HIBISCUS

1 part rum
1 tsp dry vermouth
1 tsp grenadine
juice of ½ lime of ¼ lemon

Shake well and strain into a cocktail glass.

15

LIGHT RUM

HOTCHA

2 parts rum
1 part sherry

Stir well and strain into a cocktail glass.

JACK KEARNS

1 part Bacardi
3 parts dry gin
1 dash lemon juice
1 dash sugar syrup

Shake well and strain into a cocktail glass.

MOFUCO

1 generous measure of Bacardi
1 tsp sugar
1 dash Angostura bitters
1 egg
lemon peel

Shake vigorously and strain into a medium-sized glass. Serve with a slice of lemon.

MONTMARTRE SPECIAL

2 parts Bacardi
1 part cream
1 dash grenadine

Shake well and strain into a cocktail glass. Serve with a sprinkling of nutmeg.

NAVY COCKTAIL

1 part rum
1 part sweet vermouth
1 tsp orange juice
1 dash Angostura bitters

Shake well and strain into a cocktail glass.

NEVADA

1 generous measure of Bacardi
juice of ½ grapefruit
juice of 1 lime
1 dash Angostura bitters
1 tsp sugar

Shake well and strain into a medium-sized glass.

PALM BEACH

1 part Bacardi
1 part dry gin
1 part pineapple juice

Shake well and strain into a cocktail glass.

PLANTERS

1 part light rum
1 part orange juice
1 dash lemon juice

Shake well and strain into a cocktail glass.

PLANTER'S PUNCH

4 parts light rum
1 part grenadine
2 parts lime juice
1 part orange juice
2 dashes Angostura bitters

Fill a tall glass with ice and pour in all the ingredients. Stir well and top up with soda water. Garnish with slices of orange, lime and lemon, and a cherry.

LIGHT RUM

POLYNESIA

1 part light rum
1 part passion fruit juice
juice of ½ lime
1 egg white

Shake well, strain into a medium-sized glass and serve with a slice of lime.

POOR DEAR OLD THING

2 parts Bacardi
1 part sherry
½ tsp lemon juice

Shake well and strain into a cocktail glass. Twist lemon peel over and serve.

PRESIDENT

1 generous measure of Bacardi
juice of ¼ orange
2 dashes grenadine

Shake well and strain into a cocktail glass. To make an EL PRESIDENT substitute dry vermouth for the orange juice.

RANGER

1 part light rum
1 part gin
1 part lemon juice
½ tsp sugar

Shake well and strain into a cocktail glass.

RED FLAG

1 part Bacardi
1 part dry gin

1 part lemon juice
1 part pineapple juice
1 dash grenadine

Shake well and strain into a cocktail glass. Serve with a slice of lemon and one of pineapple.

ROBSON

2 parts rum
1 part grenadine
½ tsp lemon juice
½ tsp orange juice

Shake well and strain into a cocktail glass. Twist lemon peel over and serve.

RUM COCKTAIL

3 parts rum
1 part sweet vermouth

Stir well and strain into a cocktail glass.

RUM MANHATTAN

3 parts rum
1 part sweet vermouth
1 dash orange bitters

Stir well, strain into a cocktail glass. Twist lemon peel over before serving.

RUM MARTINI

3 parts rum
1 part dry vermouth
1 dash orange bitters

Make in the same way as a RUM MANHATTAN but serve with a rinsed olive or cocktail onion.

LIGHT RUM

RUM OLD-FASHIONED

1 measure of rum
1 lump of sugar
1 dash of Angostura bitters

Add bitters to sugar in a small tumbler. Dissolve the sugar with a little soda water. Add one lump of ice and the rum, and stir.

SANTIAGO I

1 generous measure of Bacardi
2 dashes grenadine
2 dashes lemon juice

Shake well and strain into a cocktail glass. You can make this with orange or lime juice in place of the lemon.

SEVILLA

1 part rum
1 part sweet vermouth
1 piece orange peel

Shake vigorously and strain into a cocktail glass. Decorate with a slice of orange.

STANLEY

2 parts rum
2 parts gin
1 part lemon juice
1 part grenadine

Shake well and strain into a cocktail glass. Twist lemon peel over and serve.

DARK RUM

DARK RUM 40-75% Dark rum, like light rum, is distilled from molasses, and the colouring in dark Jamaican rums is produced naturally, either from burnt sugar or burnt molasses.

BOSSA NOVA

4 parts dark rum
1 part lemon juice
1 part lime juice
2 parts passion fruit juice

Shake well and strain into a medium-sized glass. Serve with crushed ice and decorate with slices of orange and lime.

QUARTER DECK

2 parts dark rum
1 part dry sherry
1 dash lime juice

Fill a small tumbler with ice and pour in the ingredients in the above order. Serve with a slice of lime. Light rum may also be used in this recipe.

RUMBA

2 parts dark rum
1 part gin
1 part light rum
1 part lemon juice
1 part lime juice
2 dashes grenadine

Shake well and strain into a tall glass. Top up with soda water, and serve with slices of lemon and lime.

RUM NOG

1 measure of dark rum
1 egg
1 level tsp sugar
1 glass milk
nutmeg to taste

Shake vigorously and strain into a tall glass. Serve with a sprinkling of nutmeg.

TRADER VIC'S PUNCH

1 part dark rum
1 part light rum
juice of ½ lemon
juice of ½ orange
1 slice pineapple
1 tsp sugar
½ tsp orgeat syrup or grenadine

Shake vigorously, or use blender, and strain into a tall glass. Serve with slices of lemon, orange and pineapple, and drink through straws.

BRANDY

BRANDY 40-50% Brandy is distilled from the fermented juice of fresh, ripe grapes. It can be made in any wine-growing country but the acknowledged king of brandies is cognac, which is a smooth full-flavoured mature blended brandy from the Charente district of France. Armagnac, which comes from the Gers region, south of Bordeaux, is another fine brandy, and good brandies are produced in Spain and Greece. A popular by-product of brandy, made from the left-over grape husks, is Marc or Grappa.

AMERICAN BEAUTY

1 part brandy
1 part dry vermouth
1 part orange juice
1 part grenadine

Shake well and strain into a cocktail glass. A dash of crème de menthe, if you have it, is optional, and some recipes suggest adding a little port.

BIG BAD WOLF

2 parts brandy
1 part orange juice
1 tsp grenadine
1 egg yolk

Shake vigorously and strain into a medium-sized glass.

BRANDY DAISY

1 part brandy
1 part lemon juice
2 dashes grenadine

Shake well and strain into a cocktail glass. This is also called a BRANDY GUMP.

BRANDY VERMOUTH

3 parts brandy
1 part sweet vermouth
1 dash Angostura bitters

Shake well and strain into a cocktail glass. If the proportions of brandy to vermouth are equal it is called a CHARLES COCKTAIL, although a CHARLES should be stirred and not shaken.

CARROL

2 parts brandy
1 part sweet vermouth

Stir well and strain into a cocktail glass. Serve with a pickled walnut or onion.

DAVIS BRANDY COCKTAIL

2 parts brandy
1 part dry vermouth
4 dashes grenadine
1 dash Angostura bitters

Stir well and strain into a cocktail glass.

BRANDY

GAZETTE

1 part brandy
1 part sweet vermouth
3 dashes lemon juice
3 dashes sugar syrup

Shake well and strain into a cocktail glass.

HARVARD

1 part brandy
1 part sweet vermouth
2 dashes Angostura bitters
1 dash sugar syrup

Stir well and strain into a cocktail glass.

HORSE'S NECK

1 generous measure of brandy
1 dash Angostura bitters
lemon peel
ginger ale

Cut a long spiral of lemon peel and loop it over the edge of a tall glass. Fill the glass with cracked ice, add the brandy and top up with ginger ale. This can also be made with gin, whisky or light rum.

JOS

1 part dry gin
1 part dry vermouth
1 part sweet vermouth
1 dash brandy
1 dash lemon or lime juice
1 dash orange bitters

Shake well and strain into a cocktail glass. Squeeze lemon peel over drink before serving.

POLONAISE

2 parts brandy
1 part dark rum
1 part dry sherry
1 part lemon juice
1 part grenadine
2 dashes Angostura bitters

Shake well and strain into a medium-sized glass.

SCORPION

1 part brandy
4 parts light rum
1 part lemon juice
2 parts orange juice
1 tsp orgeat syrup

Shake well and strain into a tumbler filled with ice cubes. Serve with a sprig of mint and a slice of orange.

SLEEPY HEAD

1 generous measure of brandy
1 piece orange peel
4 leaves fresh mint
ginger ale to top up

Shake well and strain into a tall glass. Top up with ginger ale and add ice cubes if wished.

THREE MILLERS

2 parts brandy
1 part Bacardi
1 dash lemon juice
1 tsp grenadine

Stir well and strain into a cocktail glass.

BRANDY

THUNDER

1 measure of brandy
1 egg yolk
1 tsp sugar syrup
pinch of cayenne pepper to serve

Shake well and strain into a medium-sized glass. Sprinkle cayenne pepper on top. For a THUNDER & LIGHTNING use powdered sugar instead of sugar syrup.

WALLICK'S SPECIAL

3 parts brandy
1 part cream
1 egg white

juice of ½ lime
½ tsp sugar
2 dashes grenadine

Shake well and strain into a wineglass. Without the cream this is a WATERBURY cocktail.

WASHINGTON

1 part brandy
2 parts dry vermouth
2 dashes Angostura bitters
2 dashes sugar syrup

Shake well and strain into a cocktail glass.

SCOTCH WHISKY

SCOTCH 40-60% This is either single malt made from barley, which is malted, mashed, fermented and then distilled, and which is considered too fine a drink to be used in cocktails, or blended whisky. There are four types of single malts: highland (including the famous Glenlivets and Speyside malts), Campbeltown (heavier and more smoky), Islay (heavier still, peaty, pungent and even more smoky), and lowland (gentler and smoother). All malt whisky is matured in well seasoned oak casks, often sherry ones, for at least three years and usually for longer. Blended whisky is plain grain spirit mixed with malt whisky to achieve a consistent flavour and colour.

AFFINITY

1 part Scotch
1 part dry vermouth
1 part sweet vermouth
2 dashes Angostura bitters

Stir well and strain into a cocktail glass. Squeeze lemon peel on top and serve.

ARROWHEAD

1 measure of Scotch
1 tsp dry vermouth
1 tsp sweet vermouth
1 tsp lemon juice
1 egg white

Shake well and strain into a medium-sized glass.

CAMERON

2 parts Scotch
1 part lemon juice
1 part orgeat syrup

Shake well and strain into a cocktail glass.

EXPRESS

1 part Scotch
1 part sweet vermouth
1 dash orange bitters

Stir well and strain into a cocktail glass. This is also called a HIGHLAND cocktail.

FLYING SCOT

2 parts Scotch
1 part sweet vermouth
1 dash Angostura bitters
1 dash sugar syrup

Shake well and strain into a cocktail glass.

HARRY LAUDER

1 part Scotch
1 part sweet vermouth
2 dashes grenadine

Stir well and strain into a cocktail glass.

SCOTCH WHISKY

HILDEBRANDE

1 generous measure of Scotch
1 lump of sugar
2 dashes Angostura bitters
sprig of mint

Crush the sugar with the bitters in a wineglass. Add a cube of ice, a twist of lemon peel, a slice of orange and a sprig of fresh mint, then pour in the Scotch.

KARL K KITCHEN

3 parts Scotch
1 part grape juice
4 dashes grenadine

Shake well and strain into a cocktail glass.

LEMON PIE

1 generous measure of Scotch
lemonade to top up

Stir the whisky with ice cubes in a tall glass. Top up with lemonade.

LOCH LOMOND

1 measure of Scotch
1 tsp sugar syrup
2 dashes Angostura bitters

Shake well and strain into a cocktail glass.

MAMIE TAYLOR

1 generous measure of Scotch
juice of 1 lime
ginger ale to top up

Shake well and strain into a tall glass. Top up with ginger ale.

MICKIE WALKER

3 parts Scotch
1 part sweet vermouth
1 dash lemon juice
1 dash grenadine

Shake well and strain into a cocktail glass.

NEW YORK I

1 generous measure of Scotch
1 tsp lime juice
1 heaped tsp sugar

Stir until sugar has dissolved, strain into a cocktail glass and squeeze lemon peel over.

ROB ROY

2 parts Scotch
1 part sweet vermouth
1 dash Angostura bitters

Shake well and strain into a cocktail glass. Some versions substitute dry for sweet vermouth.

SCOTS MIST

1 generous measure of Scotch

Shake with crushed ice and pour, unstrained, into a wineglass. Add a twist of lemon and serve with straws.

STONE FENCE

1 generous measure of Scotch
sugar to taste
2 dashes Angostura bitters
* (optional)*

Pour Scotch over ice into a whisky tumbler and top up with soda water. This is also known as a STONE WALL.

TENNIS GIRL

1 part Scotch
2 parts dry vermouth
1 dash lime juice

Shake well and strain into a cocktail glass.

THISTLE

1 part Scotch
1 part sweet vermouth
2 dashes Angostura bitters

Stir well and strain into a cocktail glass. Orange bitters can be substituted for the Angostura bitters, in which case halve the amount of sweet vermouth.

WEMBLEY I

1 part Scotch
1 part dry vermouth
1 part pineapple juice

Shake well and strain into a cocktail glass.

WESTBROOK

1 part Scotch
3 parts gin

1 part sweet vermouth
sugar to taste

Shake well and strain into a cocktail glass.

WHISKY SOUR

1 measure of Scotch
juice of ½ lemon
½ tsp sugar
1 tsp egg white

Shake well and strain into a medium-sized glass. The egg white may be omitted, in which case top up with soda water.

WHISKY SPECIAL

3 parts Scotch
2 parts dry vermouth
1 part orange juice
pinch of nutmeg

Shake well and strain into a medium-sized glass. Serve with an olive.

WHISPER

1 part Scotch
1 part dry vermouth
1 part sweet vermouth

Shake well and strain into a cocktail glass.

BOURBON

BOURBON 40-50%   Originally Bourbon was distilled from pure corn (maize) in Bourbon County, Kentucky. Nowadays Bourbon is made from 51 per cent corn, with rye, barley malt, wheat and oats making up the other 49 per cent.

BORDEVER

1 part Bourbon
1 part ginger ale

Stir well and strain into a cocktail glass. Twist lemon peel over and serve. This is also called a LIONEL.

BOURBON COCKTAIL

1 measure of Bourbon
1 dash orange bitters
1 dash sugar syrup
2 drops Angostura bitters

Stir well and strain into a cocktail glass.

BROWN DERBY

1 measure of Bourbon
1 tsp honey
1 tsp grapefruit juice

Shake well and strain into a cocktail glass. This is also called a DE RIGUEUR.

BUSTER BROWN

1 measure of Bourbon
1/2 tsp lemon juice
1/2 tsp sugar
2 dashes orange bitters

Shake well and strain into a cocktail glass.

CATERPILLAR

2 parts Bourbon
1 part grape juice
1 dash Angostura bitters

Shake well and strain into a cocktail glass.

COWBOY

2 parts Bourbon
1 part cream

Shake well and strain into a cocktail glass.

CROW

2 parts Bourbon
1 or 2 parts lemon juice to taste
1 dash grenadine

Shake well and strain into a cocktail glass. Twist lemon peel over and serve.

DIZZY IZZY

1 part Bourbon
1 part sherry
1 tsp pineapple juice
2 dashes lemon juice

Shake well and strain into a cocktail glass. Serve with a slice of lemon.

BOURBON

HEATHER

3 parts Bourbon
1 part dry vermouth
3 dashes orange bitters
1 dash Angostura bitters
2 dashes grenadine

Stir well and strain into a cocktail glass.

JIMMIE WALKER

3 parts Bourbon
1 part sweet vermouth
1 dash lemon juice
1 dash grenadine

Shake well and strain into a cocktail glass.

KILTIE

1 part Bourbon
1 part dry vermouth
1 dash Angostura bitters

Stir well and strain into a cocktail glass. Squeeze lemon peel over and serve. Another version may be made by substituting half the amount of sweet vermouth for the dry and 2 dashes of orange bitters for the Angostura.

LOS ANGELES

1 measure of Bourbon
1 dash sweet vermouth
1 tsp sugar
1 egg
juice of ¼ lemon

Shake vigorously and strain into a medium-sized glass.

MILAN

1 part Bourbon
1 part Bacardi
½ tsp orange juice

Shake well and strain into a cocktail glass. Twist lemon peel over and serve.

OLSON

2 parts Bourbon
1 part cream
1 tsp honey
nutmeg to serve

Shake well and strain into a cocktail glass. Add a sprinkling of nutmeg. This is also called a ONE TWO THREE.

PERFECTO

3 parts Bourbon
2 parts dry vermouth
1 part sweet vermouth
1 dash orange bitters
1 drop Angostura bitters

Stir well and strain into a medium-sized glass.

REDSKIN

2 parts Bourbon
1 part dry vermouth
2 drops Angostura bitters

Stir well and strain into a cocktail glass.

SCOTS GUARDS

1 part Bourbon
1 part lemon juice
1 part orange juice
1 tsp grenadine

BOURBON

Shake well and strain into a cocktail glass. This is also called a WARD EIGHT, when it should be served with slices of orange and lemon.

STYRRUP

2 parts Bourbon
1 part orange juice
2 drops Angostura bitters

Stir well and strain into a cocktail glass. Twist lemon peel over and serve. Decorate with a slice of orange.

WESTMINSTER

1 part Bourbon
1 part dry vermouth
1 part sweet vermouth

Shake well and strain into a cocktail glass.

WHISKY BLOSSOM

2 parts Bourbon
1 part sweet vermouth
1 dash lemon juice
1 dash pineapple juice

Shake well and strain into a cocktail glass.

RYE 40-50%   Made chiefly in the US, but also in Canada, this used to be a spirit distilled purely from rye. Nowadays, however, it is a distillation of at least 51 per cent rye with the rest made up from other grains.

BLINKER

2 parts rye
3 parts grapefruit juice
1 part grenadine

Shake well and strain into a cocktail glass.

CABLEGRAM

1 generous measure of rye
juice of ½ lemon
½ tbsp sugar
ginger ale to top up

Shake well and strain into a tall glass. Top up with ginger ale.

COMMODORE

1 generous measure of rye
juice of ½ lime
1 tsp sugar syrup
2 dashes orange bitters

Shake well and strain into a cocktail glass.

INK STREET

2 parts rye
1 part lemon juice
1 part orange juice

Shake well and strain into a cocktail glass. A less potent version has only one part rye.

MANHATTAN

2 parts rye
1 part sweet vermouth
1 dash Angostura bitters

Stir well and strain. A sweet Manhattan can be made by using equal parts of rye and sweet vermouth and omitting the Angostura bitters; a dash of orange bitters is optional. A dry Manhattan is made by substituting dry vermouth for the sweet. Manhattans can also be made with Bourbon.

MOUNTAIN

3 parts rye
1 part dry vermouth
1 part sweet vermouth
1 part lemon juice
1 egg white

Shake vigorously and strain into a large wineglass.

NEW YORK II

1 generous measure of rye
juice of ½ lime
4 dashes grenadine

Shake well and strain into a cocktail glass. Twist orange peel over and serve.

RYE

NINETEEN-TWENTY

2 parts rye
1 part dry vermouth
1 part sweet vermouth
1 dash orange bitters

Stir well and strain into a cocktail glass. Twist lemon peel over.

OLD-FASHIONED

1 generous measure of rye or
   Bourbon
2 dashes Angostura bitters
1 lump of sugar

Crush sugar with the bitters in a whisky tumbler. Add a lump of ice, a twist of lemon peel and a slice of orange. Stir in the rye or Bourbon. Brandy, gin and rum Old-fashioneds are all made in the same way.

OLD PEPPER

1 part rye
1 part Bourbon
juice of ½ lemon
1 drop Tabasco sauce
1 dash Worcestershire sauce
1 dash chilli sauce

Shake well and strain into a cocktail glass.

OPENING COCKTAIL

2 parts rye
1 part sweet vermouth
1 part grenadine

Stir well and serve in a cocktail glass with a cherry. The same drink made with Bourbon is called an OPPENHEIM.

PALMER

1 generous measure of rye
1 dash lemon juice
1 dash Angostura bitters

Shake well and strain into a cocktail glass.

QUAKER

1 part rye
1 part brandy
1 tsp raspberry syrup
juice of ½ lime

Shake well and strain into a cocktail glass.

ROCK & RYE

1 generous measure of rye
1 piece of rock candy
juice of 1 lemon (optional)

Dissolve the piece of rock in the rye and add lemon juice to taste.

RYE COCKTAIL

1 generous measure of rye
4 dashes sugar syrup
1 dash Angostura bitters

Stir well and strain into a cocktail glass. Serve with a cherry.

SCOFF-LAW

2 parts rye or Bourbon
2 parts dry vermouth
1 part lemon juice
1 part grenadine
1 dash orange bitters

Shake well and strain into a medium-sized glass.

RYE

SG

1 part rye
1 part lemon juice
1 part orange juice
1 tsp grenadine

Shake well and strain into a cocktail glass. Serve with slices of lemon and orange.

SOUL KISS II

2 parts rye
2 parts dry vermouth
1 part Dubonnet
1 part orange juice

Stir well and strain into a medium-sized glass. Serve with a slice of orange.

IRISH WHISKEY

IRISH 40% Irish whiskey is a grain spirit distilled mainly from malted barley. It differs from Scotch in that it is less smoky. This is due to the curing method of the malt; in Ireland the kilns have solid floors so that the smoke from the burning fuel doesn't come into contact with the malt. In Scotland the malted barley is smoke-cured.

BLARNEY

2 parts Irish
1 part sweet vermouth

Stir well, strain into a cocktail glass and serve with a cherry.

CAMERON'S KICK

2 parts Irish
2 parts Scotch
1 part lemon juice
1 part orgeat syrup

Shake well and strain into a medium-sized glass.

RORY O'MORE

1 part Irish
1 part sweet vermouth
1 dash Angostura bitters

Shake well and strain into a cocktail glass.

WILD EYED ROSE

2 parts Irish
1 part grenadine
juice of ½ lime

Stir with a lump of ice in a wineglass. Add a squirt of soda.

VODKA

VODKA 35-80% A colourless and unflavoured spirit, vodka can be distilled from any grain. It is the Russian national spirit and was originally distilled from the then plentiful and cheap wheat. It should be drunk quickly while it is still well-chilled.

BLOODY BULL

1 part vodka
1 part tomato juice
1 part cold beef consommé

Shake well and strain into a wine-glass. Add freshly ground black pepper to taste.

BLOODY MARY

1 part vodka
1-2 parts tomato juice
1-2 tsp lemon juice
1 dash Tabasco sauce (optional)
2 dashes Worcestershire sauce

Shake well and strain into a wine-glass. Add salt and freshly ground black pepper to taste.

BOGEY

2 parts vodka
1 part lime juice cordial
  (preferably Rose's)
ginger beer to top up

Pour over ice cubes in a tall glass and top up with ginger beer.

BULLSHOT

1 part vodka
1-2 parts cold beef consommé

Shake well and strain into a wine-glass. Add freshly ground black pepper to taste.

CHELSEA REACH

1 part vodka
1 part orange juice
medium-dry cider to top up

Pour over ice cubes in a tall glass and serve with a slice of orange.

COSSACK COOLER

1 generous measure of vodka
equal parts ginger ale and cider
to top up

Pour over ice cubes in a tall glass and serve with a slice of lemon and a sprig of mint.

SCREWDRIVER

1 park vodka
2 parts orange juice

Shake well and strain into a wine-glass. Add ice cubes and a slice of orange.

SOVIET

1 part vodka
1 part dry vermouth
1 part sherry

VODKA

Shake well and strain into a cocktail glass.

SUMMERTIME

1 part vodka
1 part dry vermouth
juice of ½ grapefruit

Pour over ice into a tall glass and top up with tonic water.

TWISTER

1 measure of vodka
1 tsp lime juice
Seven Up to top up

Pour over ice into a tall glass and top up with Seven Up.

VLADIVOSTOCK VIRGIN

2 parts vodka
2 parts dry gin
1 part grapefruit juice
1 dash Angostura bitters

Shake well and strain into a well-chilled cocktail glass. Serve with a slice of cucumber.

VODKA MARTINI

4 parts vodka
1 part dry vermouth

Stir well and strain into a cocktail glass. Serve with a twist of lemon peel. This is sometimes, rather inelegantly, referred to as a VODKATINI.

PERNOD 45% A proprietary brand of pastis which took its name from the oldest and largest firm to distil absinthe. Since the prohibition of absinthe, Pernod has been used as a substitute and it is very popular as an aperitif as well as in cocktails. It has an aniseed base and contains no wormwood. It should be drunk well-chilled and is colourless when neat but turns cloudy white when mixed with water.

ABSINTHE COCKTAIL

1 part Pernod
1 part water
1 dash sugar syrup
1 dash Angostura bitters

Shake well and strain into a cocktail glass.

APPARENT

1 part dry gin
1 part Dubonnet
1 dash Pernod

Stir well and strain into a cocktail glass.

ATOM BOMB

1 part Pernod
1 part brandy

Stir well and strain into a cocktail glass.

BLACKTHORN I

1 part Irish
1 part dry vermouth
3 dashes Pernod
3 dashes Angostura bitters

Shake well and strain into a cocktail glass.

BRAZIL

1 part dry vermouth
1 part sherry
1 dash Pernod
1 dash Angostura bitters

Stir well and strain into a cocktail glass. Twist lemon peel over and serve.

BRONX EMPRESS

1 part dry gin
1 part dry vermouth
1 part orange juice
3 dashes Pernod

Shake well and strain into a cocktail glass. Serve with a slice of orange.

BRUNELLE

1 part Pernod
3 parts lemon juice
1/2 tbsp sugar

Shake well and strain into a cocktail glass. Serve with a slice of lemon.

PERNOD

CORDOVA

2 parts dry gin
1 part sweet vermouth
1 dash Pernod
1 tsp cream

Shake well and strain into a cocktail glass.

DEEP SEA

1 part dry vermouth
1 part gin
1 dash Pernod
1 dash orange bitters

Shake well and strain into a cocktail glass. Twist lemon peel over and serve with an olive.

DIXIE

1 part Pernod
2 parts dry gin
1 part dry vermouth

Shake well and strain into a cocktail glass.

DU BARRY

1 part dry vermouth
2 parts gin
2 dashes Pernod
1 dash Angostura bitters

Shake well and strain into a cocktail glass.

DUCHESS

1 part Pernod
1 part dry vermouth
1 part sweet vermouth

Shake well and strain into a cocktail glass.

FASCINATOR

2 parts dry gin
1 part dry vermouth
2 dashes Pernod
1 sprig fresh mint

Shake well and strain into a cocktail glass.

FOURTH DEGREE

1 part dry vermouth
1 part gin
1 part sweet vermouth
4 dashes Pernod

Shake well and strain into a cocktail glass.

GASPER

1 part Pernod
1 part gin

Shake well, strain into a cocktail glass and stir in a drop of sugar syrup if desired.

GLIDER

3 parts dry gin
1 part lime juice
1 dash Pernod
2 dashes grenadine
1 egg white

Shake vigorously and strain into a medium-sized glass.

HARRY'S COCKTAIL

2 parts gin
1 part sweet vermouth
1 dash Pernod
2 sprigs mint

PERNOD

Shake well and strain into a cocktail glass. Serve with a stuffed olive.

HASTY

1 part dry vermouth
2 parts gin
1 dash Pernod
4 dashes grenadine

Shake well and strain into a cocktail glass. Halve the grenadine and you have a SAVOY FRIEND. Cut it to only 1 dash and you have a PICCADILLY.

JEYPLAK

2 parts gin
1 part sweet vermouth
1 dash Pernod

Shake well and strain into a cocktail glass. Serve with a cherry.

LONDON

1 measure of dry gin
2 dashes Pernod
2 dashes orange bitters
2 dashes sugar syrup

Stir well and strain into a cocktail glass. Twist lemon peel over and serve.

LUSITANIA

1 part brandy
2 parts dry vermouth
1 dash Pernod
1 dash orange bitters

Stir well and strain into a cocktail glass.

MACARONI

2 parts Pernod
1 part sweet vermouth

Shake well and strain into a cocktail glass.

MAIDEN'S HAIR

1 part Pernod
2 parts dry gin
1 tsp grenadine

Shake well and strain into a cocktail glass.

MAURICE

2 parts dry gin
1 part dry vermouth
1 part sweet vermouth
1 dash Pernod
juice of ¼ orange

Shake well and strain into a cocktail glass. Serve with a slice of orange.

MODERN I

1 measure of Scotch
1 dash Pernod
2 dashes rum
1 dash orange bitters
2 dashes lemon juice

Shake well and strain into a cocktail glass.

MONKEY GLAND

2 parts dry gin
1 part orange juice
3 dashes Pernod
3 dashes grenadine

PERNOD

Shake well and strain into a cocktail glass. Some recipes substitute Bénédictine for the Pernod which gives a sweeter taste.

NICK'S OWN

1 part brandy
1 part sweet vermouth
1 dash Pernod
1 dash Angostura bitters

Shake well and strain into a cocktail glass. Squeeze lemon peel over and serve with a cherry.

NINEPINE

2 parts Pernod
1 part gin
1 dash Angostura bitters
1 dash orange bitters
1 dash sugar syrup

Shake well and strain into a cocktail glass.

OLIVETTE

1 measure of gin
3 dashes Pernod
2 dashes orange bitters
2 dashes sugar syrup

Shake well and strain into a cocktail glass. Twist lemon peel over and serve with an olive.

PANSY

1 measure of Pernod
6 dashes grenadine
2 dashes Angostura bitters

Shake well and strain into a cocktail glass.

PEGGY

2 parts dry gin
1 part dry vermouth
1 dash Pernod
1 dash Dubonnet

Shake well and strain into a cocktail glass.

PHOEBE SNOW

1 part brandy
1 part Dubonnet
1 dash Pernod

Shake well and strain into a cocktail glass.

PRESTO

4 parts brandy
1 part sweet vermouth
1 part orange juice
1 dash Pernod

Shake well and strain into a medium-sized glass.

RATTLESNAKE

1 measure rye
2 dashes Pernod
1 tsp lemon juice
1/2 tsp sugar
1/2 egg white

Shake well and strain into a medium-sized glass.

SAZERAC

1 generous measure of rye
1 lump of sugar
1 dash Angostura bitters
1 dash Pernod

Crush the sugar lump with the rye, the bitters and some crushed ice. Strain into a well-chilled cocktail glass, add the Pernod and twist lemon peel over before serving.

THIRD DEGREE

1 part dry vermouth
2 parts gin
4 dashes Pernod

Stir well and strain into a cocktail glass.

TNT

1 part Pernod
1 part rye

Shake well and strain into a cocktail glass.

VICTORY

1 part Pernod
1 part grenadine

Shake well and strain into a wineglass. Top up with soda water.

WHIZZ BANG

1 part dry vermouth
2 parts Scotch
2 dashes Pernod
2 dashes orange bitters
2 dashes grenadine

Shake well and strain into a cocktail glass.

YOKOHAMA

2 parts dry gin
1 part vodka
2 parts orange juice
1 part grenadine
1 dash Pernod

Shake well and strain into a medium-sized glass. Like vodka cocktails, all Pernod cocktails should be served well-chilled in cold glasses.

CURAÇAO

CURAÇAO 25-40% This is a liqueur made from the peel of bitter green oranges which grow on Curaçao in the West Indies. Other ingredients include rum, port wine, brandy and spices. It comes in several colours – orange is the most popular, but also green, white and blue – however this does not affect the flavour.

BARON

2 parts dry gin
1 part dry vermouth
6 dashes Curaçao
2 dashes sweet vermouth

Shake well and strain into a cocktail glass.

BERRY WALL

1 part dry gin
1 part sweet vermouth
4 dashes Curaçao

Shake well and strain into a cocktail glass. Twist lemon peel over before serving.

BLUE BIRD

1 measure of gin
5 dashes orange Curaçao
4 dashes Angostura bitters

Shake well and strain into a cocktail glass.

BOMBAY

2 parts brandy
1 part dry vermouth
1 part sweet vermouth
2 dashes Curaçao
1 dash Pernod

Shake well and strain into a cocktail glass.

BOOSTER

1 generous measure of brandy
4 dashes Curaçao
1 egg white

Shake well and strain into a medium-sized glass. Serve with a sprinkling of nutmeg.

BOSOM CARESSER

1 part Curaçao
2 parts brandy
1 tsp grenadine
1 egg yolk

Shake vigorously and strain into a medium-sized glass.

BRANDY COCKTAIL

1 part Curaçao
3 parts brandy

Stir well and strain into a cocktail glass.

CANADIAN COCKTAIL

1 measure of Curaçao
3 dashes rum (light or dark)
juice of ¼ lemon
1 tsp sugar

Shake well and strain into a cocktail glass.

CHURCH PARADE

1 part dry vermouth
2 parts gin
1 dash orange Curaçao
4 dashes orange juice

Shake well and strain into a cocktail glass.

DAMN-THE-WEATHER

2 parts gin
1 part sweet vermouth
1 part orange juice
3 dashes Curaçao

Shake well and strain into a cocktail glass.

DREAM

1 part Curaçao
2 parts brandy
1 dash Pernod

Shake well and strain into a cocktail glass.

EAST INDIA

1 part orange Curaçao
6 parts brandy
1 part pineapple juice
1 dash Angostura bitters

Stir well and strain into a cocktail glass.

FAIR & WARMER

2 parts Bacardi
1 part sweet vermouth
2 dashes Curaçao

Shake well and strain into a cocktail glass.

FOX TROT

1 generous measure of Bacardi
2 dashes orange Curaçao
juice of 1 lime or ½ lemon

Shake well and strain into a cocktail glass.

GREEN ROOM

1 part brandy
2 parts dry vermouth
2 dashes Curaçao

Shake well and strain into a cocktail glass.

GUARD'S

2 parts dry gin
1 part sweet vermouth
2 dashes Curaçao

Shake well and strain into a cocktail glass.

HAKAM

1 part dry gin
1 part sweet vermouth
2 dashes Curaçao
1 dash orange bitters

Shake well and strain into a cocktail glass.

HAWAIIAN

1 part Curaçao
2 parts gin
1 part orange juice

CURAÇAO

Shake well and strain into a cocktail glass. This is also called a HOULA HOULA.

JOURNALIST

1 part dry vermouth
4 parts gin
1 part sweet vermouth
2 dashes Curaçao
1 dash Angostura bitters
2 dashes lemon juice

Shake well and strain into a medium-sized glass.

MAIDEN'S BLUSH

1 generous measure of dry gin
4 dashes orange Curaçao
4 dashes grenadine
1 dash lemon juice

Shake well and strain into a cocktail glass.

MORNING GLORY

1 part brandy
1 part rye
3 dashes Curaçao
3 dashes Pernod
3 dashes sugar syrup
2 dashes orange bitters

Stir well and strain into a medium-sized glass. Top up with soda water, twist lemon peel over and serve.

NEWBURY

1 part dry gin
1 part sweet vermouth
3 dashes Curaçao
1 piece lemon peel
1 piece orange peel

Shake vigorously and strain into a cocktail glass.

OLYMPIC

1 part Curaçao
1 part brandy
1 part orange juice

Shake well and strain into a cocktail glass. Serve with a slice of orange.

PANTHER'S BREATH

1 part Curaçao
1 part cream

In the given order so that the cream floats on top, pour the ingredients carefully into a well-chilled sherry glass. Add a dash of Angostura bitters.

PEGU CLUB

1 part Curaçao
2 parts gin
1 tsp lime juice
1 dash Angostura bitters
1 dash orange bitters

Shake well and strain into a cocktail glass.

SANTIAGO II

1 part orange Curaçao
2 parts Bacardi
1 part lime juice
2 dashes Angostura bitters

Pour ingredients over ice into a medium-sized glass, stir and serve with a wedge of orange.

SATAN'S CURLY WHISKERS

1 part orange Curaçao
2 parts dry vermouth
2 parts gin
2 parts sweet vermouth
2 parts orange juice
1 dash orange bitters

Shake well and strain into a medium-sized glass. Serve with a slice of orange.

SIR WALTER

1 part brandy
1 part rum
1 tsp Curaçao
1 tsp grenadine
1 tsp lemon juice

Shake well and strain into a cocktail glass. Serve with a slice of lemon.

SNYDER

2 parts dry gin
1 part dry vermouth
3 dashes Curaçao

Shake well and strain into a cocktail glass. Twist orange peel over and serve.

SOUTHERN GIN

1 generous measure of dry gin
2 dashes Curaçao
2 dashes orange bitters

Shake well and strain into a cocktail glass.

TANGO

2 parts dry gin
1 part dry vermouth
1 part sweet vermouth
2 dashes Curaçao
juice of ¼ orange

Shake well and strain into a cocktail glass. Serve with a slice of orange.

TEN-FIFTEEN

1 part Curaçao
1 part dry vermouth
1 part cream
nutmeg to taste

Shake well and strain into a cocktail glass. Sprinkle nutmeg over and serve.

VERMOUTH & CURACAO

1 part Curaçao
3 parts dry vermouth

Stir well and strain into a wineglass. Top up with soda and add one ice cube. This can also be served neat in a cocktail glass.

WEESUER SPECIAL

1 part orange Curaçao
1 part dry gin
1 part dry vermouth
1 part sweet vermouth
4 dashes Pernod

Shake well and strain into a cocktail glass. Twist orange peel over and serve.

CURAÇAO

WHIP

2 parts brandy
1 part dry vermouth
1 part sweet vermouth
3 dashes Curaçao
1 dash Pernod

Shake well and strain into a cocktail glass.

WILL ROGERS

1 part dry vermouth
2 parts gin
1 part orange juice
4 dashes Curaçao

Shake well and strain into a cocktail glass. Either twist orange peel over the drink before serving, or decorate with an orange slice.

YOUNG MAN

3 parts brandy
1 part sweet vermouth
2 dashes Curaçao
1 dash Angostura bitters

Shake well and strain into a cocktail glass. Serve with an olive or a cherry.

APRICOT BRANDY

APRICOT BRANDY 20-40% True apricot brandy is distilled from fresh apricots and their crushed kernels. The finest comes from Hungary and is strong at 40%. But apricot brandy is also the name given to the liqueur made by infusing dried apricots in a spirit base. If brandy is the spirit used then the results taste that much better. This form of apricot brandy is less strong at 20-35%.

ABBEY BELLS

2 parts apricot brandy
1 part dry vermouth
4 parts gin
1 part orange juice
1 dash grenadine

Shake well and strain into a cocktail glass.

AFTER SUPPER

1 part apricot brandy
1 part Curaçao
4 dashes lemon juice

Shake well and strain into a cocktail glass.

APPLE PIE II

1 part Bacardi
1 part sweet vermouth
4 dashes apricot brandy
2 dashes grenadine
4 dashes lemon juice

Shake well and strain into a cocktail glass.

APRICOT COCKTAIL

2 parts apricot brandy
1 part lemon juice
1 part orange juice
1 dash dry gin

Shake well and strain into a cocktail glass.

APRICOT LADY

4 parts apricot brandy
4 parts light rum
1 part orange Curaçao
2 parts lime juice
½ egg white

Shake well and strain into a medium-sized glass. Serve with a slice of orange and drink through straws.

BULL FROG

1 generous measure of apricot
   brandy
juice of 1 lemon

Shake well and strain into a cocktail glass. Decorate with a slice of lemon.

BUTLER

1 part dry gin
1 part pineapple juice
3 dashes apricot brandy

Shake well and strain into a cocktail glass.

APRICOT BRANDY

CUBAN COCKTAIL II

1 part apricot brandy
2 parts brandy
juice of ½ lime or ¼ lemon

Shake well and strain into a cocktail glass. Serve with a slice of lime or lemon.

DARB

1 part apricot brandy
1 part dry gin
1 part dry vermouth
4 dashes lemon juice

Shake well and strain into a cocktail glass.

DOLLY O'DARE

1 part dry gin
1 part dry vermouth
6 dashes apricot brandy

Shake well and strain into a cocktail glass. Twist orange peel over and serve.

FAIRY BELLE

1 part apricot brandy
3 parts dry gin
1 egg white
1 tsp grenadine

Shake well and strain into a medium-sized glass.

FAVOURITE

1 part apricot brandy
1 part dry gin
1 part dry vermouth
1 dash lemon juice

Shake well, strain into a cocktail glass and add a dash of grenadine. Serve it with a cherry and you have a FAIRBANKS.

GOODNIGHT LADIES

1 part apricot brandy
3 parts dry gin
1 part grenadine
1 part lemon juice

Shake well and strain into a cocktail glass.

GRADEAL SPECIAL

1 part apricot brandy
2 parts Bacardi
1 part dry gin

Shake well and strain into a cocktail glass.

HOP TOAD

3 parts apricot brandy
1 part lemon juice

Shake well and strain into a cocktail glass.

KATINKA

2 parts apricot brandy
3 parts vodka
1 part lime juice

Shake well and strain into a cocktail glass. Serve with crushed ice and a sprig of mint.

KITCHEN SINK

1 part apricot brandy
1 part gin

APRICOT BRANDY

1 part rye
1 part lemon juice
1 part orange juice
1 egg
½ tsp sugar

Shake vigorously and strain into a medium-sized glass.

LEAVE IT TO ME

1 part apricot brandy
1 part dry vermouth
2 parts gin
1 dash lemon juice
1 dash grenadine

Shake well and strain into a cocktail glass. Increase the quantity of grenadine to 4 dashes and you have an ENGLISH ROSE, sometimes called a WESTERN ROSE.

LUTKINS SPECIAL

1 part dry gin
1 part dry vermouth
2 dashes apricot brandy
2 dashes orange juice

Shake well and strain into a cocktail glass. Serve with a slice of orange.

PARADISE

1 part apricot brandy
2 parts gin
1 part orange juice
1 dash lemon juice

Shake well and strain into a cocktail glass. Serve with a slice of orange.

PRINCESS

2 parts apricot brandy
1 part sweetened cream

In the given order so that the cream floats on top, pour the ingredients carefully into a well-chilled cocktail glass.

RESOLUTE

1 part apricot brandy
2 parts dry gin
1 part lemon juice

Shake well and strain into a cocktail glass.

SPENCER

1 part apricot brandy
2 parts dry gin
1 dash Angostura bitters
1 dash orange juice

Shake well and strain into a cocktail glass. Twist orange peel over and serve with a cherry

SWEET DREAMS

2 parts apricot brandy
1 part gin
2 parts light rum
1 part pineapple juice
2 parts cream

Shake vigorously or blend. Strain into a medium-sized glass and serve with a twist of orange peel.

TOBY SPECIAL

1 part apricot brandy
1 part Bacardi
1 part grenadine
1 part lemon juice

APRICOT BRANDY

Shake well and strain into a cocktail glass.

VALENCIA

2 parts apricot brandy
1 part orange juice
4 dashes orange bitters

Shake well and strain into a cocktail glass.

WEBSTER

1 part apricot brandy
2 parts dry vermouth
4 parts gin
1 part lime juice

Shake well and strain into a cocktail glass.

ZOMBIE

2 parts apricot brandy
2 parts dark rum
2 parts light rum
1 part lemon juice
1 part orange juice
1 part pineapple juice

Shake well, strain and pour over crushed ice into a tall glass. Serve with a slice of orange, lemon, lime, and pineapple, and a cherry.

COINTREAU 40% This is the most famous and most refined form of triple sec orange Curacao. It is a colourless drink with a pronounced orange flavour.

ACAPULCO

2 parts Cointreau
4 parts light rum
1 part lime juice
½ egg white
½ tsp sugar

Shake well and strain into a tall glass. Top up with soda water and serve with a sprig of mint, a slice of lemon, and two straws.

ALPINE GLOW

1 part Cointreau
4 parts brandy
4 parts dark rum
2 parts lemon juice
2 dashes grenadine

Shake vigorously, strain and serve in a tall glass with a slice of lemon, a sprig of mint and a cherry.

BALALAIKA

1 part Cointreau
2 parts vodka
1 part lemon juice

Shake well and strain into a cocktail glass. Squeeze lemon peel over and serve with a twist of orange peel.

BEAUTIFUL

1 part Cointreau
2 parts Bacardi
2 parts dark rum
2 parts lemon juice
1 part grenadine

Shake well and strain into a medium-sized glass.

BETWEEN THE SHEETS

1 part Cointreau
1 part brandy
1 part light rum
1 part lemon or lime juice

Shake well and strain into a cocktail glass.

BIG BOY

1 part Cointreau
2 parts brandy
1 part lemon syrup

Shake well and strain into a cocktail glass.

BLUE MONDAY

1 part Cointreau
3 parts vodka
1 dash blue vegetable extract

Shake well and strain into a cocktail glass.

COINTREAU

BLUE TRAIN

1 part Cointreau
2 parts dry gin
1 part lemon juice
1 dash blue vegetable extract

Shake well and strain into a cocktail glass.

CHURCHILL

1 part Cointreau
3 parts Scotch
1 part sweet vermouth
1 part lime juice

Shake well and strain into a cocktail glass.

CLARIDGE

1 part Cointreau
1 part apricot brandy
2 parts dry gin
2 parts dry vermouth

Shake well and strain into a cocktail glass.

COINTREAU ROCKS

1 very generous measure of
  Cointreau
3 dashes Angostura bitters

Pour the Cointreau over ice cubes into a small tumbler, add the bitters and serve with a slice of lemon.

DANDY

1 part Dubonnet
1 part rye
3 dashes Cointreau
1 dash Angostura bitters

1 piece of lemon peel
1 piece of orange peel

Shake vigorously and strain into a cocktail glass.

DESHLER

1 part Dubonnet
1 part rye
2 dashes Cointreau
2 dashes orange bitters
1 piece of lemon peel
1 piece of orange peel

Shake well and strain into a cocktail glass. Twist lemon peel over and serve.

DODGE SPECIAL

1 part Cointreau
1 part gin
1 dash grape juice

Shake well and strain into a cocktail glass.

FINE & DANDY

1 part Cointreau
2 parts gin
1 part lemon juice
1 dash Angostura bitters

Shake well and strain into a cocktail glass.

FRANKENJACK

1 part Cointreau
1 part apricot brandy
2 parts dry vermouth
2 parts gin

Shake well and strain into a cocktail glass.

HOUR GLASS

1 part Cointreau
1 part brandy
1 part Pernod

Shake well and strain into a medium-sized glass. Add a lump of ice, top up with soda water, twist lemon peel over and serve.

LITTLE DEVIL

1 part Cointreau
2 parts Bacardi
2 parts dry gin
1 part lemon juice

Shake well and strain into a cocktail glass.

MAHJONG

1 part Cointreau
1 part Bacardi
4 parts dry gin

Shake well and strain into a cocktail glass.

MAIDEN'S PRAYER

3 parts Cointreau
3 parts dry gin
1 part lemon juice
1 part orange juice

Shake well and strain into a cocktail glass.

NEWTON SPECIAL

1 part Cointreau
3 parts brandy
1 dash Angostura bitters

Shake well and strain into a cocktail glass.

ORANGE BLOOM

1 part Cointreau
2 parts dry gin
1 part sweet vermouth

Shake well and strain into a cocktail glass. Serve with a cherry.

ORANGE FIZZ

1 generous measure of gin
2 tsp Cointreau
2 tbsp lemon juice
2 dashes orange bitters
1 1/2 tbsp sugar syrup

Shake well and strain into a medium-sized glass. Add ice and top up with soda water. Twist orange peel over and serve with a slice of orange.

QUEEN ELIZABETH

1 part Cointreau
2 parts dry gin
1 part lemon juice
1 dash Pernod

Shake well and strain into a cocktail glass. Serve with a slice of lemon.

SHERRY TWIST

1 part Cointreau
1 part brandy
1 part dry vermouth
3 parts sherry
1 dash lemon juice
cinnamon to taste

Shake well and strain into a medium-sized glass. Sprinkle with a little cinnamon before serving.

COINTREAU

SIDECAR

1 part Cointreau
2 parts brandy
1 part lemon juice

Shake well and strain into a cocktail glass.

SUNSET IN PARADISE

1 part Cointreau
4 parts dark rum
1 part sweet vermouth
2 parts lime juice
1 tsp brown sugar

Shake vigorously and strain into a medium-sized glass. Serve with a twist of orange and a cherry.

SWEET PATOOTIE

1 part Cointreau
2 parts dry gin
1 part orange juice

Shake well and strain into a cocktail glass.

THIS IS IT

1 part Cointreau
2 parts gin
1 part lemon juice
1 egg white

Shake well and strain into a medium-sized glass.

TREBLE CHANCE

1 part Cointreau
1 part dry vermouth
1 part Scotch

Stir well and strain quickly into a cocktail glass.

ULANDA

1 part Cointreau
2 parts dry gin
1 dash Pernod

Shake well and strain into a cocktail glass.

UP TOWN

2 parts dark rum
1 part lime juice
1 part orange juice
1 part pineapple juice
1 dash Cointreau
1 dash Angostura bitters
1 dash grenadine

Shake well and strain into a tall glass. Serve with straws and decorate with a slice of lime, orange and pineapple, and a cherry.

WHITE BABY

1 part Cointreau
2 parts gin
1 part lemon syrup

Shake well and strain into a cocktail glass.

WHITE LADY

1 part Cointreau
2 parts dry gin
1 part lemon juice

Shake well and strain into a cocktail glass.

WHITE LILY

1 part Cointreau
1 part Bacardi
1 part gin
1 dash Pernod

Shake well and strain into a cocktail glass.

XYZ

1 part Cointreau
2 parts Bacardi
1 part lemon juice

Shake well and strain into a cocktail glass.

ZA ZA

1 part Cointreau
2 parts gin
1 part sweet vermouth
orange juice to top up

Pour over crushed ice in a tall glass. Top up with orange juice and decorate with slices of orange and lemon.

APPLE BRANDY

APPLE BRANDY 45-50% A colourless spirit distilled from cider, also known as applejack. Calvados is the best, and most famous, apple brandy. It is made in Normandy and is well matured in oak casks.

ANGEL FACE

1 part apple brandy
1 part apricot brandy
1 part dry gin

Shake well and strain into a cocktail glass.

APPLE COCKTAIL

2 parts apple brandy
1 part brandy
1 part gin
2 parts sweet cider

Shake well and strain into a medium-sized glass.

APPLEJACK

1 part apple brandy
1 part sweet vermouth
1 dash Angostura bitters

Shake well and strain into a cocktail glass.

APPLEJACK RABBIT

3 parts apple brandy
1 part lemon juice
1 part orange juice
½ tsp maple syrup

Shake well and strain into a wineglass. Add ice cubes. The rim of the glass may be dipped in maple syrup and then coated with sugar, in which case some recipes call for lime juice in place of the orange.

APPLEJACK SPECIAL

4 parts apple brandy
1 part lemon juice
1 part grenadine

Shake well and strain into a cocktail glass.

BENTLEY

1 part apple brandy
1 part Dubonnet

Shake well and strain into a cocktail glass.

BLOCK & FALL

1 part apple brandy
2 parts brandy
2 parts Cointreau
1 part Pernod

Shake well and strain into a cocktail glass.

CALVADOS COCKTAIL

2 parts apple brandy (Calvados should be used)
1 part Cointreau
2 parts orange juice
1 part orange bitters

Shake well and strain into a cocktail glass.

CORPSE REVIVER

1 part apple brandy
2 parts brandy
1 part sweet vermouth

Shake well and strain into a cocktail glass.

DEAUVILLE

1 part apple brandy
1 part brandy
1 part Cointreau
1 part lemon juice

Shake well and strain into a cocktail glass.

DEPTH CHARGE I

4 parts apple brandy
4 parts brandy
3 parts lemon juice
1 part grenadine

Shake well and strain into a medium-sized glass.

EMPIRE

1 part apple brandy
1 part apricot brandy
2 parts gin

Shake well and strain into a cocktail glass.

GOLDEN DAWN

1 part apple brandy
1 part apricot brandy
1 part dry gin
1 part orange juice
1 dash grenadine

Shake all the ingredients except the grenadine and strain them into a well-chilled glass rinsed in the grenadine. Some recipes omit the grenadine altogether, easier perhaps but not so pretty.

JACK ROSE

2 parts apple brandy
1 part lime juice
1 part grenadine

Shake well and strain into a cocktail glass.

JERSEY LIGHTNING

1 part apple brandy
2 parts brandy
1 part sweet vermouth
1 dash Angostura bitters

Shake well and strain into a cocktail glass.

KICKER

1 part apple brandy
1 part Bacardi
2 dashes sweet vermouth

Shake well and strain into a cocktail glass.

LEEWARD

1 part apple brandy
2 parts light rum
1 part sweet vermouth

Shake well and strain into a medium-sized glass filled with crushed ice. Serve with a twist of lemon.

APPLE BRANDY

LIBERTY

2 parts apple brandy
1 part Bacardi
1 dash sugar syrup

Shake well and strain into a cocktail glass.

MANETTI

1 part apple brandy
1 part Cointreau
1 part gin
2 parts cream
1 dash grenadine
1 dash lemon juice

Shake vigorously and strain into a medium-sized glass.

PRINCE'S SMILE

1 part apple brandy
1 part apricot brandy
2 parts dry gin
1 dash lemon juice

Shake well and strain into a cocktail glass.

ROYAL SMILE

2 parts apple brandy
1 part dry gin
1 part grenadine
juice of ¼ lemon

Shake well and strain into a cocktail glass.

SAUCY SUE

1 part apple brandy
1 part brandy
1 dash apricot brandy
1 dash Pernod

Stir well and strain into a cocktail glass. Twist orange peel over before serving.

SHARKY PUNCH

3 parts apple brandy
1 part rye
1 tsp sugar syrup

Shake well and strain into a medium-sized glass. Top up with soda water. Serve with a slice of apple.

SONORA

1 part apple brandy
1 part Bacardi
2 dashes apricot brandy
1 dash lemon juice

Shake well and strain into a cocktail glass. Serve with a slice of lemon.

SO-SO

1 part apple brandy
2 parts dry gin
2 parts sweet vermouth
1 part grenadine

Shake well and strain into a cocktail glass. Serve with a slice of apple.

SPECIAL ROUGH

1 part apple brandy
1 part brandy
1 dash Pernod

Shake well and strain into a well-chilled cocktail glass.

APPLE BRANDY

STAR I

1 part apple brandy
1 part dry gin
1 dash dry vermouth
1 dash sweet vermouth
1 tsp grapefruit juice

Shake well and strain into a cocktail glass.

STAR II

1 part apple brandy
1 part sweet vermouth

Shake well and strain into a cocktail glass.

THIRD RAIL

1 part apple brandy
1 part Bacardi
1 part brandy
1 dash Pernod

Shake well and strain into a cocktail glass.

TORPEDO

2 parts apple brandy
1 part brandy
1 dash gin

Shake well and strain into a cocktail glass.

TULIP

2 parts apple brandy
1 part apricot brandy
2 parts sweet vermouth
1 part lemon juice

Shake well and strain into a cocktail glass.

TUNNY

2 parts apple brandy
1 part dry gin
2 dashes Pernod
1 dash sugar syrup

Stir well and strain into a cocktail glass.

WEMBLEY II

2 parts dry gin
1 part dry vermouth
2 dashes apple brandy
1 dash apricot brandy

Shake well and strain into a cocktail glass.

WHIST

2 parts apple brandy
1 part Bacardi
1 part sweet vermouth

Shake well and strain into a cocktail glass.

WHOOPEE

1 part apple brandy
1 part brandy
1 part Pernod

Stir well and strain quickly into a well-chilled cocktail glass.

WOODSTOCK

2 parts apple brandy
1 part dry vermouth

Stir well and strain quickly into a cocktail glass.

BENEDICTINE

BENEDICTINE 43% The oldest liqueur, first made in 1510 by the Bénédictine Abbey of Fécamp in Normandy. It is beautifully sweet and smooth and is made from a cognac base with a secret recipe containing 27 herbs and spices.

BOBBY BURNS

1 part Scotch
1 part sweet vermouth
3 dashes Bénédictine

Shake well and strain into a cocktail glass. Twist lemon peel over and serve.

BRAINSTORM

1 generous measure of Irish
2 dashes Bénédictine
2 dashes dry vermouth

Stir well and strain into a cocktail glass. Twist orange peel over and serve.

CHRYSANTHEMUM

1 part Bénédictine
2 parts dry vermouth
3 dashes Pernod

Shake well and strain into a cocktail glass. Twist orange peel over and serve.

FROUPE

1 part brandy
1 part sweet vermouth
3 dashes Bénédictine

Stir well and strain into a cocktail glass.

GIPSY

1 part Bénédictine
2 parts vodka
1 dash Angostura bitters

Shake well and strain into a cocktail glass.

HONEYMOON

1 part Bénédictine
1 part apple brandy
3 dashes Curaçao
juice of ½ lemon

Shake well and strain into a cocktail glass.

MERRY WIDOW

1 part dry gin
1 part dry vermouth
2 dashes Bénédictine
2 dashes Pernod
2 dashes Angostura bitters

Stir well and strain into a cocktail glass. Twist lemon peel over.

OH HENRY

1 part Bénédictine
1 part Bourbon
1 part ginger ale

Stir well and strain into a cocktail glass.

POET'S DREAM

2 parts dry gin
1 part dry vermouth
2 dashes Bénédictine
2 dashes orange bitters

Shake well and strain into a cocktail glass.

ROLLS ROYCE

2 parts dry gin
1 part dry vermouth
1 part sweet vermouth
1 dash Bénédictine

Shake well and strain into a cocktail glass.

WIDOW'S DREAM

1 measure of Bénédictine
1 egg
cream to top up

Shake the Bénédictine and the egg vigorously and strain into a medium-sized glass. Float cream on top, carefully to keep it in a separate layer.

SWEDISH PUNCH

SWEDISH PUNCH 30% This is a form of rum or arrack flavoured with tea and lemon.

BIFFY

1 part Swedish punch
2 parts dry gin
1 part lemon juice

Shake well and strain into a cocktail glass.

BOOMERANG

1 part Swedish punch
1 part dry vermouth
1 part rye
1 dash Angostura bitters
1 dash lemon juice

Shake well and strain into a cocktail glass.

CFH

1 part Swedish punch
1 part apple brandy
2 parts gin
1 part lemon juice
1 part grenadine

Shake well and strain into a medium-sized glass.

DEVONSHIRE PRIDE

1 part Swedish punch
2 parts apply brandy
1 dash lemon juice

Shake well and strain into a cocktail glass.

DIKI DIKI

1 part Swedish punch
4 parts apple brandy
1 part grapefruit juice

Shake well and strain into a cocktail glass. Serve with a slice of apple.

DOCTOR

2 parts Swedish punch
1 part lime or lemon juice

Shake well and strain into a cocktail glass. Serve with a slice of lime or lemon.

FULL HOUSE

1 part Swedish punch
2 parts Bacardi
1 part dry vermouth

Shake well and strain into a cocktail glass. Add a dash of grenadine and you have a FOUR FLUSH cocktail.

GRAND SLAM

2 parts Swedish punch
1 part dry vermouth
1 part sweet vermouth

Shake well and strain into a cocktail glass.

SWEDISH PUNCH

HAVANA

1 part Swedish punch
2 parts apricot brandy
1 part dry gin
1 dash lemon juice

Shake well and strain into a cocktail glass.

HESITATION

3 parts Swedish punch
1 part rye
1 dash lemon juice

Shake well and strain into a cocktail glass.

HUNDRED PER CENT

4 parts Swedish punch
1 part lemon juice
1 part orange juice
2 dashes grenadine

Shake well and strain into a cocktail glass.

MELBA

1 part Swedish punch
1 part Bacardi
2 dashes Pernod
2 dashes grenadine
juice of ½ lime or ¼ lemon

Shake well and strain into a cocktail glass.

ROULETTE

1 part Swedish punch
2 parts apple brandy
1 part Bacardi

Shake well and strain into a cocktail glass.

TANGLEFOOT

2 parts Swedish punch
2 parts Bacardi
1 part lemon juice
1 part orange juice

Shake well and strain into a medium-sized glass.

TWELVE MILES OUT

1 part Swedish punch
1 part apple brandy
1 part Bacardi

Shake well and strain into a cocktail glass. Twist orange peel over and serve.

WALDORF

2 parts Swedish punch
1 part dry gin
1 part lemon juice

Shake well and strain into a cocktail glass.

WELCOME STRANGER

1 part Swedish punch
1 part brandy
1 part gin
1 part lemon juice
1 part orange juice

Shake well and strain into a cocktail glass.

MARASCHINO

MARASCHINO 30-40%   A cherry liqueur originally made in Dalmatia from Marasca cherries and their stones. It is now made in many other countries. It has a drier and more sophisticated taste than cherry brandy.

FRENCH ROSE

1 part Maraschino or cherry
   brandy
2 parts dry gin
1 part dry vermouth

Shake well and strain into a cocktail glass. Twist lemon peel over before serving.

OLYMPIA

2 parts rum
1 part lime juice
1 tsp Maraschino or cherry
   brandy

Stir well and strain into a cocktail glass.

OPERA

1 part Maraschino
4 parts dry gin
1 part Dubonnet

Shake well and strain into a cocktail glass. Twist orange peel over before serving.

PETO

1 part dry vermouth
2 parts gin
1 part sweet vermouth
2 dashes Maraschino
juice of ¼ orange

Shake well and strain into a cocktail glass. Serve with a slice of orange.

POUSSE L'AMOUR

1 part Maraschino
1 egg yolk
1 part Bénédictine
1 part brandy

In the given order so that they do not blend together, pour the ingredients carefully into a well-chilled sherry glass.

SARATOGA

1 generous measure of brandy
2 dashes Maraschino
2 dashes Angostura bitters
¼ slice of pineapple

Shake vigorously and strain into a medium-sized glass. Top up with soda water.

SENSATION

3 parts dry gin
3 dashes Maraschino
1 part lemon juice
3 sprigs mint

Shake well and strain into a cocktail glass.

MARASCHINO

SILVER

1 part dry gin
1 part dry vermouth
2 dashes Maraschino
2 dashes orange bitters

Shake well and strain into a cocktail glass. Twist orange peel over and serve.

SINGAPORE SLING

1 part Maraschino or cherry
* brandy*
1 part gin
1 part lemon juice
1 tsp sugar

Shake well and strain into a tall glass. Top up with soda water. Twist lemon peel over and serve with a cherry.

SNICKER

2 parts dry gin
1 part dry vermouth
2 dashes Maraschino
1 dash orange bitters
1 tsp sugar syrup
1 egg white

Shake well and strain into a medium-sized glass.

TURF

1 part dry vermouth
1 part gin
2 dashes Maraschino
2 dashes Pernod
2 dashes orange bitters

Shake well and strain into a cocktail glass.

TUXEDO

1 part dry gin
1 part dry vermouth
1 dash Maraschino
1 dash Pernod
2 dashes orange bitters

Shake well and strain into a cocktail glass. Twist lemon peel over.

VANDERBILT

2 parts Maraschino
2 parts brandy
1 part lemon juice
2 dashes Angostura bitters
2 dashes sugar syrup

Stir well and strain into a cocktail glass. Serve with a twist of lemon.

WHITE PLUSH

1 part Maraschino
2 parts dry gin
½ pint milk

Shake well and strain into a well-chilled tumbler.

WILLIE SMITH

1 part Maraschino
2 parts brandy
1 dash lemon juice

Shake well and strain into a cocktail glass.

YORK SPECIAL

1 part Maraschino
3 parts dry vermouth
4 dashes orange bitters

Shake well and strain into a cocktail glass.

LILLET

LILLET 17% A bitter sweet vermouth-like aperitif the colour of a sweet white wine. It is made from white wine and Armagnac.

ABBEY

1 part Lillet
2 parts dry gin
1 part orange juice
1 dash Angostura bitters

Shake well and strain into a cocktail glass.

CAMPDEN

1 part Lillet
1 part Cointreau
2 parts dry gin

Shake well and strain into a cocktail glass.

CULROSS

1 part Lillet
1 part apricot brandy
1 part Bacardi
1 part lemon juice

Shake well and strain into a cocktail glass.

DEPTH CHARGE II

1 part Lillet
1 part dry gin
2 dashes Pernod

Shake well and strain into a cocktail glass. Twist orange peel over before serving.

EDDIE BROWN

1 part Lillet
2 parts dry gin
2 dashes apricot brandy

Shake well and strain into a cocktail glass. Twist lemon peel over before serving.

H & H

1 part Lillet
2 parts dry gin
2 dashes Curaçao

Shake well and strain into a cocktail glass. Twist orange peel over before serving.

HOOPLA

1 part Lillet
1 part brandy
1 part Cointreau
1 part lemon juice

Shake well and strain into a cocktail glass. Twist lemon peel over before serving.

HOOTS MON

1 part Lillet
2 parts Scotch
1 part sweet vermouth

Stir well and strain into a cocktail glass.

LILLET

JIMMY BLANC

1 part Lillet
2 parts dry gin
3 dashes Dubonnet

Shake well and strain into a cocktail glass. Twist orange peel over before serving.

KINA

1 part Lillet
2 parts dry gin
1 part sweet vermouth

Shake well and strain into a cocktail glass.

PURITAN

1 part Lillet
1 part gin
1 dash apricot brandy
2 dashes orange juice

Shake well and strain into a cocktail glass. Twist lemon peel over before serving.

RICHMOND

1 part Lillet
2 parts gin

Stir well and strain into a cocktail glass. Twist lemon peel over before serving. Add a dash of Angostura bitters and omit the lemon zest and you have a GREAT SECRET.

SELF STARTER

2 parts Lillet
1 part apricot brandy
3 parts dry gin
2 dashes Pernod

Stir well and strain into a cocktail glass.

WEDDING BELLS I

2 parts Lillet
1 part Curaçao
2 parts rye
1 part orange bitters

Stir well with ice in a medium-sized glass.

WEDDING BELLS II

1 part Lillet
2 parts orange Curaçao
3 parts rye
1 dash orange bitters

Stir well with ice in a medium-sized glass.

CREME DE CACAO

CREME DE CACAO 25-30% A perennial favourite in cocktails, this is a chocolate and vanilla flavoured liqueur made from cocoa beans. It comes in brown and white and is generally used in sweet after-dinner drinks.

ANGEL'S TIP

3 parts crème de cacao
1 part cream

Pour the crème de cacao into a liqueur glass and float cream on top. This is a KING ALPHONSE if the cream is sweetened.

BARBARA

1 part crème de cacao
2 parts vodka
1 part cream

Shake well and strain into a cocktail glass.

BRANDY ALEXANDER

1 part crème de cacao
1 part brandy
1 part cream

Shake well and strain into a cocktail glass.

FIFTH AVENUE

1 part crème de cacao
1 part apricot brandy
1 part sweetened cream

In the given order so that they remain in separate layers, pour the ingredients carefully into a liqueur glass.

GOLDEN GATE

1 part crème de cacao
4 parts dark rum
2 parts gin
1 part lemon juice
a pinch of ginger

Shake vigorously and strain into a whisky tumbler.

POPPY

1 part crème de cacao
2 parts dry gin

Shake well and strain into a cocktail glass.

PRINCESS MARY

1 part crème de cacao
1 part gin
1 part cream (sweetened to taste)

Shake well and strain into a cocktail glass. Sprinkle a little nutmeg over before serving.

RUSSIAN COCKTAIL

1 part crème de cacao
1 part gin
1 part vodka

Shake well and strain into a cocktail glass.

CREME DE CACAO

SARABANDE

1 part crème de cacao
1 part gin
2 parts orange juice
1 part cream
½ egg white

Shake vigorously, or blend if possible, and strain into a tall glass.

SAVOY COCKTAIL

1 part crème de cacao
1 part Bénédictine
1 part brandy

In the given order so that they remain in separate layers, pour the ingredients carefully into a liqueur glass.

TROPICAL

1 part crème de cacao
1 part dry vermouth
1 part Maraschino
1 dash Angostura bitters
1 dash orange bitters

Shake well and strain into a cocktail glass.

GREEN CHARTREUSE

GREEN CHARTREUSE 55% This is another ancient herbal liqueur distilled by monks. The secret recipe is said to contain 130 different herbs and spices and has been perfected by the Carthusian brothers since the sixteenth century.

BIJOU

1 part green Chartreuse
1 part gin
1 part sweet vermouth
1 dash orange bitters

Stir well and strain into a cocktail glass.

BITER

1 part green Chartreuse
2 parts gin
1 part lemon juice (sweetened to taste)
1 dash Angostura bitters

Shake well and strain into a cocktail glass.

GREEN-EYED MONSTER

1 part green Chartreuse
1 part dry gin
1 part sweet vermouth

Stir well and strain into a cocktail glass.

JERSEY

1 part green Chartreuse
1 part brandy

In the given order so that they remain in layers, pour the ingredients carefully into a liqueur glass.

JERSEY LILY

2 parts green Chartreuse
1 part brandy
10 drops Angostura bitters

Make in the same way as a JERSEY and add the bitters before serving.

ST GERMAIN

1 measure of green Chartreuse
juice of ¼ grapefruit
juice of ½ lemon
1 egg white

Shake well and strain into a medium-sized glass.

SAND MARTIN

1 part dry gin
1 part sweet vermouth
1 tsp green Chartreuse

Stir well and strain into a cocktail glass.

SPRING FEELING

1 part green Chartreuse
2 parts gin
1 part lemon juice

Shake well and strain into a cocktail glass.

GREEN CHARTREUSE

TIPPERARY I

1 part green Chartreuse
1 part Irish
1 part sweet vermouth

Shake well and strain into a cocktail glass.

UNION JACK

1 part grenadine
1 part Maraschino
1 part green Chartreuse

In the given order so that they remain in separate layers, pour the ingredients carefully into a liqueur glass. The colours of this cocktail bear no relation to any known flag.

WIDOW'S KISS

1 part green Chartreuse
2 parts apple brandy
1 part Bénédictine
1 dash Angostura bitters

Shake well and strain into a cocktail glass.

ZARAGOZANA

1 part apricot brandy
1 part Bénédictine
1 part green Chartreuse
1 part Cointreau
1 part cognac
1 part crème de cacao

In the given order pour ingredients over shaved ice into a sherry glass.

GREEN CREME DE MENTHE

GREEN CREME DE MENTHE 25-30% A sweet, peppermint flavoured liqueur made from brandy and fresh mint, popular in after-dinner drinks.

APRÈS SKI

1 part green crème de menthe
1 part Pernod
1 part vodka
lemonade to top up

Shake well and strain into a tall glass. Top up with lemonade and serve with a slice of lemon, sprig of mint and straws.

CARUSO

1 part green crème de menthe
1 part dry gin
1 part dry vermouth

Shake well and strain into a cocktail glass.

CUCUMBER

1 part green crème de menthe
1 part sweetened cream

Pour crème de menthe into a liqueur glass and carefully float cream on top.

EVERYBODY'S IRISH

1 generous measure of Irish
3 dashes green crème de menthe
6 dashes green Chartreuse

Shake well and strain into a cocktail glass. Serve with a green olive.

FALLEN ANGEL

1 generous measure of dry gin
2 dashes green crème de menthe
1 dash Angostura bitters
juice of ½ lime

Shake well and strain into a cocktail glass.

FLORIDA

1 part green crème de menthe
4 parts Bacardi
1 part lemon juice
1 part pineapple juice

Shake well and strain into a tall glass. Top up with soda water.

GRASSHOPPER

1 part green crème de menthe
1 part crème de cacao

In the given order so that they remain in separate layers, pour the ingredients carefully into a liqueur glass. This can also be made with cream if you use white crème de cacao. Pour equal parts of all three ingredients into your mixer, shake well and strain.

GREEN CREME DE MENTHE

JADE

1 part green crème de menthe
2 parts light rum
1 part orange Curaçao
1 part lime juice

Shake well and strain into a cocktail glass. Serve with a slice of lime. This can also be served as a long drink on the rocks with soda.

PLAYING FIELDS

1 small measure of dry gin
1 tsp green crème de menthe
1 dash Angostura bitters
ginger beer to top up

Stir in a tumbler. Add cracked ice and top up with ginger beer.

SHAMROCK

1 part dry vermouth
1 part Irish
3 dashes green crème de menthe
3 dashes green Chartreuse

Shake well and strain into a cocktail glass.

STARBOARD LIGHT

1 part green crème de menthe
2 parts dry gin
1 part lemon juice

Shake well and strain into a cocktail glass. Serve with a slice of lemon.

WHITE CREME DE MENTHE

WHITE CREME DE MENTHE 25-30%   White and green crème de menthe taste identical but in some cocktails the vivid green colour might look a little disconcerting, so the use of white crème de menthe is recommended.

CASTLE DIP

1 part white crème de menthe
1 part apple brandy
3 dashes Pernod

Shake well and strain into a cocktail glass.

COLD DECK

1 part white crème de menthe
2 parts brandy
1 part sweet vermouth

Shake well and strain into a cocktail glass.

ETHEL

1 part white crème de menthe
1 part apricot brandy
1 part Curaçao

Shake well and strain into a cocktail glass.

KNOCK-OUT

1 part dry gin
1 part dry vermouth
1 part Pernod
1 tsp white crème de menthe

Shake well and strain into a cocktail glass, which should be well-chilled.

STINGER

1 part white crème de menthe
3 parts brandy

Shake well and strain into a cocktail glass.

WHITE SPIDER

1 part white crème de menthe
1 park vodka

Shake well and strain into a cocktail glass.

WHITE WINGS

1 part white crème de menthe
2 parts dry gin

Shake well and strain into a cocktail glass.

GRAND MARNIER

GRAND MARNIER 35-40% A delicious French liqueur made from champagne cognac and orange Curaçao.

ALFONSO I

2 parts Grand Marnier
1 part dry gin
1 part dry vermouth
4 dashes sweet vermouth
1 dash Angostura bitters

Shake well and strain into a cocktail glass.

BARTENDER

1 part dry vermouth
1 part Dubonnet
1 part gin
1 part sherry
1 dash Grand Marnier

Stir well and strain into a cocktail glass.

GLOOM CHASER

1 part Grand Marnier
1 part Curaçao
1 part lemon juice
1 part grenadine

Shake well and strain into a cocktail glass.

IOLANTHE

1 part Grand Marnier
2 parts brandy
2 parts Lillet
1 part orange juice
3 dashes orange bitters

Shake well and strain into a cocktail glass.

LARCHMONT

2 parts Grand Marnier
4 parts Bacardi
1 part lime juice

Shake well and strain into a whisky tumbler with ice. Serve with a twist of orange peel.

LEAP YEAR

1 part Grand Marnier
4 parts gin
1 part sweet vermouth
1 dash lemon juice

Shake well and strain into a cocktail glass. Twist lemon peel over before serving.

LORRAINE

1 part Grand Marnier
2 parts gin
1 part Lillet

Stir well and strain into a cocktail glass.

MARNY

1 part Grand Marnier
2 parts dry gin

Shake well and strain into a cocktail glass.

GRAND MARNIER

SATAN'S WHISKERS

1 part Grand Marnier
2 parts dry vermouth
2 parts gin
2 parts sweet vermouth
2 parts orange juice
1 dash orange bitters

Shake well and strain into a
medium-sized glass. See also
SATAN'S CURLY WHISKERS.

UP-TO-DATE

1 part rye
1 part sherry
2 dashes Grand Marnier
2 dashes Angostura bitters

Shake well and strain into a cocktail glass.

VAN DUSEN

2 parts dry gin
1 part dry vermouth
2 dashes Grand Marnier

Stir well and strain into a cocktail
glass.

YANKEE PRINCE

1 part Grand Marnier
3 parts dry gin
juice of ¼ orange

Shake well and strain into a cocktail glass.

SLOE GIN 25%   This is not a true gin at all but is a liqueur made from sloe berries macerated in gin. It is a dark reddish purple and very sweet. It improves greatly with keeping; ten years after bottling it is delicious.

BLACKTHORN II

1 part sloe gin
1 part sweet vermouth
2 dashes orange bitters

Stir well and strain into a cocktail glass. Twist orange peel over and serve.

BLACKTHORN III

1 part sloe gin
1 part dry vermouth
1 part sweet vermouth
1 dash orange bitters
2 drops Angostura bitters

Stir well and strain into a cocktail glass. Twist lemon peel over before serving.

ECLIPSE

2 parts sloe gin
1 part dry gin
grenadine

Pour enough grenadine into a cocktail glass to cover a ripe olive. Mix the gins together and pour carefully over the grenadine so that they do not blend with it, but remain in separate layers. Twist orange peel over before serving or decorate with a slice of orange.

EXPOSITION

1 part sloe gin
1 part dry vermouth
1 part Maraschino or cherry
  brandy

Shake well and strain into a cocktail glass.

FAIR & WARM

1 part sloe gin
1 part Dubonnet
1 part sherry
1 dash Bénédictine

Shake well and strain into a cocktail glass.

JOHNNIE MACK

2 parts sloe gin
1 part orange Curaçao
3 dashes Pernod

Shake well and strain into a cocktail glass. If you do not have orange Curaçao you can make a McCLELLAND by using any other Curaçao and cutting the Pernod to only one dash.

MABEL BERRA

1 part sloe gin
1 part Swedish punch
juice of ½ lime

SLOE GIN

Shake well and strain into a cocktail glass.

MILLIONAIRE II

1 part sloe gin
1 part apricot brandy
1 part rum
1 dash grenadine
juice of 1 lime

Shake well and strain into a cocktail glass.

MODERN II

2 parts sloe gin
1 part Scotch
1 dash Pernod
1 dash orange bitters
1 dash grenadine

Shake well and strain into a cocktail glass.

MOLL

1 part sloe gin
1 part gin
1 dash orange bitters
1 dash lemon juice
½ tsp sugar

Shake well and strain into a cocktail glass.

PING PONG I

4 parts sloe gin
1 part dry vermouth
1 part sweet vermouth

Stir well and strain into a cocktail glass. If you halve the quantity of sloe gin you have a SLOE GIN COCKTAIL.

PING PONG II

1 part sloe gin
1 part sweet vermouth
2 dashes Curacao
2 drops Angostura bitters

Shake well and strain into a cocktail glass.

RUGBY

2 parts sloe gin
1 part dry vermouth
2 parts gin
1 part sweet vermouth
2 dashes Bénédictine

Shake well and strain into a cocktail glass.

SAVOY TANGO

1 part sloe gin
1 part apple brandy

Shake well and strain into a cocktail glass.

SILVER FLASH

2 parts sloe gin
1 part Bénédictine
1 dash orange bitters

Shake well and strain into a cocktail glass.

SLOEBERRY

1 generous measure of sloe gin
1 dash Angostura bitters
1 dash orange bitters

Shake well and strain into a cocktail glass.

TIPPERARY II

2 parts sloe gin
1 part dry vermouth
1 dash lemon juice

Shake well and strain into a cocktail glass. Twist lemon peel over and serve.

TRADE WINDS

1 part sloe gin
4 parts light rum
1 part lime juice
1 tsp sugar

Shake well and strain into a wineglass with crushed ice.

DRAMBUIE

DRAMBUIE 40% The Oldest Scots liqueur. It is sweet and smooth and is said to be made to Bonnie Prince Charlie's own recipe of malt whisky, heather honey, and herbs.

BONNIE PRINCE CHARLIE

1 part Drambuie
2 parts brandy
2 parts lemon juice

Shake well and strain into a cocktail glass.

BONNIE SCOT

1 part Drambuie
2 parts Scotch
1 part lemon juice

Shake well and strain into a cocktail glass.

BRITISH FESTIVAL

1 part Drambuie
2 parts gin
1 part lime juice

Shake well and strain into a cocktail glass.

EMBASSY ROYAL

1 part Drambuie
1 part Bourbon
1 part sweet vermouth
2 dashes orange juice

Shake well and strain into a cocktail glass. Serve with a twist of orange peel.

PRINCE EDWARD

1 part Drambuie
2 parts dry vermouth
4 parts Scotch

Shake well and strain into a whisky tumbler. Top up with soda water and serve with a slice of orange and a cherry.

RUSTY NAIL

1 part Drambuie
1 part Scotch

Stir well and strain into a cocktail glass. This is sometimes served on the rocks in a whisky tumbler.

ST ANDREW'S

1 part Drambuie
1 part Scotch
1 part orange juice

Shake well and strain into a cocktail glass.

SCOTS KILT

1 part Drambuie
2 parts Scotch
2 dashes orange bitters

Stir well and strain into a cocktail glass. Serve with a twist of orange peel.

CREME DE NOYAU

CREME DE NOYAU(X) 25-30% A sweet, almond-tasting liqueur. It is either pink or colourless and is made from the crushed kernels of peaches, apricots and cherries.

JOCKEY CLUB

1 generous measure of dry gin
2 dashes crème de noyau
1 dash Angostura bitters
1 dash orange bitters
4 dashes lemon juice

Shake well and strain into a cocktail glass.

LILY

1 part crème de noyau
1 part dry gin
1 part Lillet
1 dash lemon juice

Shake well and strain into a cocktail glass.

OLD ETONIAN

1 part gin
1 part Lillet
2 dashes crème de noyau
2 dashes orange bitters

Shake well and strain into a cocktail glass. Twist orange peel over before serving. Substitute sloe gin for ordinary gin and you have a SLOE MEASURE.

PINK SQUIRREL

1 part crème de noyau
1 part crème de cacao (preferably white)
1 part cream

Shake vigorously and strain into a cocktail glass.

TEQUILA

TEQUILA 40% A colourless, strong, dryish drink, double distilled from mescal, or maguey sap. The maguey is a cactus-like plant, a kind of aloe. It is increasingly popular thanks to Margaritas.

BROADWAY THIRST

2 parts Tequila
1 part lemon juice
1 part orange juice
1 tsp sugar syrup

Shake well and strain into a cocktail glass.

MAI TAI

1 part Tequila
2 parts apricot brandy
1 part Cointreau
1 part dark rum
2 parts light rum
1 part orange juice
2 dashes Angostura bitters
2 dashes grenadine
1 dash orgeat syrup

Shake vigorously or blend and strain into a medium-sized glass. Serve with a slice of orange, lemon and lime.

MARGARITA

2 parts Tequila
1 part Cointreau
1 part lime or lemon juice
    (or half and half)

Shake well and strain into a cocktail glass with a salt-frosted rim. To frost the rim of the glass first moisten its inner and outer edges with a wedge of lemon, then dip the rim in a saucer of fine salt, coating it evenly. Shake off any excess.

TEQUADOR

4 parts Tequila
1 part lime juice
5 parts pineapple juice
3 drops grenadine

Shake the Tequila with the fruit juices and pour over crushed ice into a tall glass. Add more crushed ice and drip the grenadine on top.

TEQUILA SUNRISE

2 parts Tequila
4 parts orange juice
1 part grenadine

Pour Tequila into a whisky tumbler filled with ice cubes, top up with orange juice and add the grenadine.

VIVA MARIA

4 parts Tequila
1 part Maraschino
2 parts lime juice
1/2 egg white
1/2 tsp grenadine

Shake well and strain into a wineglass filled with crushed ice.

CREME DE CASSIS

CREME DE CASSIS 25% A sweet, blackcurrant, French liqueur made from brandy, blackcurrants and sugar. The best comes from the Dijon area.

BROADWAY SMILE

1 part crème de cassis
1 part Swedish punch
1 part Cointreau

In the given order so that they remain in separate layers, pour the ingredients carefully into a liqueur glass.

MISSISSIPPI MULE

1 part crème de cassis
4 parts dry gin
1 part lemon juice

Shake well and strain into a cocktail glass.

PARISIAN

1 part crème de cassis
1 part dry vermouth
1 part gin

Shake well and strain into a cocktail glass.

STARS & STRIPES

1 part crème de cassis
1 part Maraschino
1 part green Chartreuse

In the given order so that they remain in layers, pour the ingredients carefully into a liqueur glass.

SUNSHINE

1 part Bacardi
1 part dry vermouth
2 dashes crème de cassis
juice of 1/4 lemon

Shake well and strain into a cocktail glass.

VERMOUTH CASSIS

1 part crème de cassis
2-4 parts dry vermouth

Pour over ice cubes into a whisky tumbler and top up with soda water. The proportions of dry vermouth to cassis may be altered to taste.

KIRSCH

KIRSCH 45% A completely clear, fruit brandy made from the juice of wild cherries and their stones. It comes mainly from Germany and Switzerland.

ALBERTINE

1 part kirsch
1 part Chartreuse
1 part Cointreau
3-5 drops Maraschino

Shake well and strain into a cocktail glass. You may use either green or yellow Chartreuse in this recipe.

CUMPARASITA

1 part kirsch
4 parts apricot brandy
4 parts brandy
1 part dry vermouth
4 parts orange juice
4 parts cream
1 dash grenadine

Fill a tall glass with ice and stir in all the ingredients except the grenadine. Add the grenadine on top and serve with straws and a slice of orange.

ETON BLAZER

1 part kirsch
3 parts gin
juice of ½ lemon
½ tbsp

Shake well and strain into a tall glass. Top up with soda.

GOAT'S DELIGHT

1 part kirsch
1 part brandy
1 dash Pernod
1 dash orgeat syrup
½ tsp cream

Shake well and strain into a cocktail glass.

JUSTINE

1 part kirsch
1 part crème de noyau
2 parts vodka
2 parts cream
2 dashes orgeat syrup

Shake vigorously and strain into a medium-sized glass.

KGB

1 part kirsch
3 parts dry gin
1 dash Angostura bitters
1 dash lemon juice

Shake well and strain into a cocktail glass.

NINETEEN

1 part kirsch
1 part dry gin
4 parts dry vermouth
1 dash Pernod
4 dashes sugar syrup

Shake well and strain into a cocktail glass, which should be well-chilled.

PINK ALMOND

1 part kirsch
1 part crème de noyau
2 parts Scotch
1 part lemon juice
1 part orgeat syrup

Shake well and strain into a cocktail glass.

VIE ROSE

2 parts kirsch
2 parts dry gin
1 part lemon juice
1 part grenadine

Shake well and strain into a cocktail glass.

YELLOW CHARTREUSE

YELLOW CHARTREUSE 40% This, like green Chartreuse, is made by the Carthusian monks, and follows an equally complex and secret recipe, but it is a sweeter and less potent liqueur.

ALASKA

1 part yellow Chartreuse
3 parts dry gin

Shake well and strain into a cocktail glass.

CLUB

2 parts dry gin
1 part sweet vermouth
1 dash yellow Chartreuse

Shake well and strain into a cocktail glass.

FOUR SCORE

1 part yellow Chartreuse
3 parts brandy
2 parts Lillet

Stir well and strain into a cocktail glass. Serve with s twist of lemon peel.

HONG KONG FIZZ

1 part yellow Chartreuse
1 part Bénédictine
1 part gin
1 part green Chartreuse
1 part vodka
1 part lemon juice

Shake vigorously and pour into a tall glass. Top up with soda and serve with a slice of orange, lemon, lime and a cherry.

SHANGHAI GIN FIZZ

1 part yellow Chartreuse
1 part Bénédictine
1 part gin
1 part lemon juice

Shake vigorously and strain into a tall glass. Top up with soda and serve with a slice of lemon, a cherry and straws.

THREEQUARTER BACK

1 part yellow Chartreuse
1 part Curaçao
1 part brandy

In the given order so that they remain in separate layers, pour the ingredients carefully into a liqueur glass.

YELLOW PARROT

1 part yellow Chartreuse
1 part apricot brandy
1 part Pernod

Shake well and strain into a cocktail glass.

CREME DE BANANE

CREME DE BANANE 25-30% A sweet, banana flavoured liqueur with a brandy base.

BANANA BLISS

2 parts crème de banane
2 parts Bacardi
2 parts cream
1 part orange juice
1 dash Angostura bitters
3-5 drops grenadine

Shake all the ingredients except the grenadine and strain into a whisky glass. Add the grenadine.

BANJINO

1 part gin
1 part orange juice
1 dash of crème de banane

Shake well and strain into a cocktail glass.

ORACABESSA

2 parts crème de banane
2 parts dark rum
1 part lemon juice
½ sliced banana to decorate
lemonade to top up

Shake well and pour into a tall glass. Add the sliced banana, top up with lemonade.

SILVER JUBILEE

1 part crème de banane
1 part gin
1 part cream

Shake well and strain into a small tumbler. Serve with a few slices of banana if wished.

SINFUL SADIE

1 part crème de banane
4 parts light rum
1 part orange juice
½ egg white
½ tsp grenadine

Shake vigorously or blend. Strain into a wine glass and serve with a slice of lime.

YELLOW FINGERS I

1 part crème de banane
2 parts crème de cassis
2 parts gin
1 part cream

Shake well and strain into a wineglass. Serve with a few slices of banana if possible.

GALLIANO

GALLIANO 40%   A sweet, golden liqueur flavoured with vanilla, herbs and spices. It is named after an Italian war hero of the 1890s. Galliano is becoming more and more popular thanks to Harvey Wallbangers.

FREDDY FUDPUCKER

1 generous measure of Tequila
orange juice to top up
Galliano

Fill a whisky tumbler with ice, add the Tequila and top up with orange juice leaving half an inch for the Galliano. Float the Galliano carefully on the top.

GOLDEN CADILLAC

2 parts Cointreau
2 parts crème de cacao (white)
2 parts cream
1 part orange juice
2 dashes Galliano

Shake vigorously and strain into a medium-sized glass.

HARVEY WALLBANGER

1 generous measure of vodka
orange juice to top up
Galliano

This is the cocktail from which the FREDDY FUDPUCKER is derived. Fill a tumbler with ice, add the vodka and the orange juice. Float the Galliano carefully on top.

MANDARIN

1 part Galliano
2 parts apricot brandy
2 parts Bénédictine
2 parts orange Curaçao
4 parts orange juice
2 parts cream

Shake vigorously and strain into a tall glass. Serve with a slice of orange.

ORANGE BLOSSOM II

1 part Galliano
2 parts apricot brandy
2 parts vodka
1 part orange juice
ginger ale to top up

Shake well and strain into a tall glass. Top up with ginger ale and serve with a slice of orange and two straws.

SUNRISE

1 part Galliano
1 part crème de banane
4 parts Tequila
1 part cream
1 dash grenadine
1 dash lemon juice

Shake well and strain into a wineglass.

TIA MARIA

TIA MARIA 30%   A Jamaican coffee liqueur. Tia Maria is rum based and is drier and more potent than Kahlua.

BLACK RUSSIAN

*1 part Tia Maria (or this can be
    made with Kahlua)*
2 parts vodka
Coca Cola to top up

Pour over ice into a whisky tumbler and stir. This can also be made using equal parts of Tia Maria and vodka and omitting the Coca Cola. See also WHITE RUSSIAN, which can be made with Coca Cola instead of cream.

CARA SPOSA

1 part Tia Maria
1 part orange Curaçao
1 part cream

Shake vigorously or blend and strain into a wineglass with a sugar-frosted rim. To frost the rim of a glass with sugar first moisten it with egg white then dip it in castor (finely granulated) sugar to coat it evenly. Shake off any excess.

LEROY WASHINGTON

1 part Tia Maria
2 parts brandy
1 part Drambuie
2 parts cream

Shake well and strain into a medium-sized glass.

VELVET HAMMER

1 part Tia Maria
1 part brandy
2 parts Cointreau
2 parts cream

Shake well and strain into a medium-sized glass.

ZIA MARIA

2 parts Tia Maria
1 part orange Curaçao
2 parts cream
1 dash Galliano

Shake well and strain into a medium-sized glass filled with crushed ice.

KAHLUA

KAHLUA 26·5%   A mexican coffee liqueur made from coffee beans, cocoa beans, vanilla and brandy.

DIZZY DAME

1 part Kahlua
1 part brandy
1 part cream
1 dash Maraschino or cherry
  brandy

Shake well and strain into a cocktail glass.

KAHLUA KISS

1 generous measure of Kahlua
1 dash crème de noyau
cream

Into a wineglass filled with crushed ice pour the Kahlua, add the crème de noyau and float cream on top.

WHITE RUSSIAN

1 part Kahlua
1 part vodka
1 part cream

Pour the vodka over ice into a wineglass. Add the Kahlua and top with cream. See also BLACK RUSSIAN.

XAVIERA

1 part Kahlua
1 part crème de noyau
1 part orange Curaçao
2 parts cream

Shake well and strain into a wineglass. Add crushed ice.

CAMPARI 24% A translucent dark red Italian aperitif with a strong, dry quinine taste.

AMERICANO

1 part Campari
2 parts sweet vermouth

Pour into a wineglass with a lump of ice. Top up with soda, stir and add a twist of lemon peel.

LONDINO

1 part Campari
1 part apricot brandy
2 parts dry vermouth
2 parts gin
1 part orange juice

Shake well and strain into a medium-sized glass.

NEGRONI

1 part Campari
1 part gin
1 part sweet vermouth

Stir well and strain into a cocktail glass. Serve with a twist of orange peel. This is one of the most popular of the classic cocktails.

OLD PAL

1 part Campari
1 part dry vermouth
1 part rye

Stir well and strain into a cocktail glass.

WINDSOR ROSE

1 part Campari
2 parts Dubonnet
3 parts gin
1 dash crème de noyau

Stir well and strain into a cocktail glass.

KUMMEL

KUMMEL 35-40% A highly-distilled, grain based liqueur, Kummel is flavoured with caraway and cumin seeds, fennel and other herbs and spices. It comes mainly from Holland or Germany and the different brands vary in sweetness but it is always pure white.

ALICE MINE

1 part kümmel
1 part sweet vermouth
2 dashes Scotch

Shake well and strain into a cocktail glass.

ALLIES

1 part dry gin
1 part dry vermouth
2 dashes kümmel

Shake well and strain into a cocktail glass.

GREEN DRAGON

1 part kümmel
2 parts crème de menthe
4 parts dry gin
1 part lemon juice
4 dashes peach bitters

Shake well and strain into a medium-sized glass.

JOHN WOOD

1 part kümmel
2 parts Irish
4 parts sweet vermouth
2 parts lemon juice
1 dash Angostura bitters

Shake well and strain into a medium-sized glass. Serve with a slice of lemon.

QUELLE VIE

1 part kümmel
2 parts brandy

Stir well and strain into a cocktail glass.

SILVER STREAK

1 part kümmel
1 part dry gin

Shake well and strain into a cocktail glass.

AMER PICON

AMER PICON 21%   A vermouth-like, French aperitif, it is slightly bitter as is indicated by the name. Amer Picon is flavoured with orange and gentian.

BROOKLYN

2 parts rye
1 part dry vermouth
1 dash Amer Picon
1 dash Maraschino

Shake well and strain into a cocktail glass.

CREOLE

1 part rye
1 part sweet vermouth
2 dashes Amer Picon
2 dashes Bénédictine

Stir well and strain into a cocktail glass. Twist lemon peel over and serve.

PICON

1 part Amer Picon
1 part sweet vermouth

Shake well and strain into a cocktail glass.

PICON & GRENADINE

2 parts Amer Picon
1 part grenadine

Pour over ice into a medium-sized glass, top up with soda and serve with a slice of orange. If you add an egg white, shake well and strain the ingredients before topping up with soda, you have an AMER PICON FIZZ.

SANCTUARY

1 part Amer Picon
1 part Cointreau
2 parts Dubonnet

Shake well and strain into a cocktail glass.

SOUTHERN COMFORT

SOUTHERN COMFORT 50%   This is the oldest American liqueur. It has a whisky and brandy base, flavoured with peaches, oranges and herbs.

RHETT BUTLER

2 parts Southern Comfort
2 parts orange Curaçao
1 part lemon juice
1 part lime juice

Shake well and strain into a tall glass filled with crushed ice. Top up with soda and serve with a slice of orange and sprig of mint. Drink through straws.

YELLOW FINGERS II

2 parts Southern Comfort
1 part Galliano
2 parts vodka
2 parts orange juice
lemonade to top up

Shake well and strain into a tall glass. Top up with lemonade and serve with a slice of orange.

EXOTIC RECIPES

ALFONSO II

1 measure sweet vermouth
1/2 tsp sugar
2 dashes Angostura bitters
champagne to top up

Half fill a tall glass with ice and
add the vermouth together with
the sugar and the bitters. Stir well
then top up with champagne.
Serve with a twist of lemon.

BELLINI

1 generous measure of peach
juice
champagne to top up

Put the peach juice in a blender
with 6 cubes of ice and blend until
the ice is crushed roughly. Pour
into a large wineglass, top up
with champagne and serve with a
peach slice.

BLACK VELVET

1 part champagne
1 part Guinness

In a well-chilled, large wineglass
pour, simultaneously, the champagne and the Guinness; do not
stir. The ingredients should also
be well chilled.

BLUE BLAZER

1 glass Scotch
1 tsp sugar

Heat two large mugs. Dissolve the
sugar in boiling water in one of
them, and in the other set fire to
the pre-heated Scotch. Pour in-

gredients from one mug to the
other in a stream of liquid fire.
Then pour into a heated wineglass, add a twist of lemon peel
and serve. Rum or brandy can
also be used in this recipe.

BUCK'S FIZZ

3 parts champagne
1 part orange juice

Fill a large wineglass with crushed
ice, add the orange juice then top
up with champagne. Serve with a
slice of orange.

CALIFORNIA DREAMING

1 generous measure pineapple
juice
2 dashes kirsch
1 dash lemon juice
champagne to top up

Put the kirsch in a blender with
the pineapple and lemon juice
and 5 cubes of ice and blend for
10 seconds. Pour into a large
wineglass and top up with champagne. Serve with a slice of pineapple and 2 straws.

CHAMPAGNE COCKTAIL

1 generous measure of champagne
1 sugar lump
1 dash Angostura bitters

Put the sugar lump in a well-
chilled wineglass and drop the
bitters onto it. Add well-chilled
champagne and serve without
stirring.

EXOTIC RECIPES

CUBAN PEACH

4 parts light rum
4 parts peach brandy
1 part lime juice
¼ tsp sugar

Shake well and strain into a wine-glass half-filled with crushed ice. Serve with a sprig of mint if wished.

FRUIT DAIQUIRI

2 parts dark rum
1 part fruit liqueur of your choice
2 parts light rum
2 parts orange juice
2 oz fruit of your choice

Blend with 6 cubes of ice and pour into a large wineglass. Drink through straws.

HENRY SPECIAL

2 parts brandy
4 parts grapefruit juice
1 part lemon juice
2 tsp honey
champagne to top up

Blend with 4 ice cubes for 20 seconds. Pour into a large wine-glass and top up with champagne.

KIR

1 part crème de cassis
7 parts dry white wine

Pour well-chilled wine into a wineglass and add crème de cassis, stirring gently.

KIR ROYALE

7 parts champagne
1 part crème de cassis

This is made in the same way as ordinary KIR but be careful not to overstir.

MAXIM'S À LONDRES

4 parts brandy
1 part Cointreau
1 part orange juice
champagne to top up

Stir all the ingredients well and strain into a chilled wineglass. Top up with champagne and serve with a slice of orange.

NEW ORLEANS DANDY

2 parts light rum
1 part peach brandy
1 dash lime juice
1 dash orange juice
champagne to top up

Shake well and strain into a large wineglass. Top up with champagne and serve with a slice of orange.

PINACOLADA

1 part Bacardi
1 part pineapple juice
2 tsp coconut milk or flesh
2 dashes Angostura bitters
1 pinch salt

Blend with 5 ice cubes until smooth. Pour into a large wine-glass and serve with a slice of pineapple and a cherry. This is a drink which doesn't really travel as it needs to be made with fresh coconut.

PINK CHEVROLET

1 measure fraise
2 oz fresh strawberries
1 dash lemon juice
champagne to top up

Blend with 3 ice cubes until smooth. Pour into a wineglass, top up with champagne and serve with a fresh strawberry.

PORT IN A STORM

1 part brandy
4 parts light red wine
3 parts port

Stir well with ice in a large wineglass. Serve with a slice of orange and lemon and a sprig of mint.

POUSSE CAFÉ I

1 part Bénédictine
1 part Curaçao
1 part kirsch

In the given order so that they remain in separate layers, pour the ingredients carefully into a liqueur glass. Special Pousse Café glasses are available for these cocktails.

POUSSE CAFÉ II

1 part yellow Curaçao
1 part kirsch
1 part green Chartreuse
1 part brandy

In the given order so that they remain in separate layers, pour the ingredients carefully into a liqueur glass.

POUSSE CAFÉ III

1 part grenadine
1 part Maraschino
1 part green crème de menthe
1 part yellow Chartreuse
1 part Curaçao
1 part brandy

In the given order so that they remain in separate layers, pour the ingredients carefully into a liqueur glass. There are recipes for Pousse Café calling for different numbers of ingredients. Here are three to try in gradual degrees of complexity.

RESTORATION

1 part brandy
1 part framboise
4 parts red wine
1 dash lemon juice

Stir ingredients with ice in a large wineglass. Top up with soda and serve with a couple of fresh raspberries if possible.

SOUTHERN PEACH

1 part peach brandy
1 part Southern Comfort
1 part cream
1 dash Angostura bitters

Shake well and strain into a wineglass. Serve with a slice of fresh peach.

EXOTIC RECIPES

STRAWBERRY CREAM COOLER

2 parts gin
1 part lemon juice
3 parts cream
*2 oz strawberries, fresh, frozen
    or tinned*
1 tsp sugar

Blend without ice for 10 seconds. Pour into a large wineglass and add a squirt of soda water and some ice cubes. Serve with a fresh strawberry and two straws.

STRAWBERRY DREAM

4 parts fraise
1 part kirsch
2 parts light rum
4 parts cream

Shake well with ice and strain into a wineglass. Serve with straws.

BIBLIOGRAPHY

The following books are all admirable and will be found useful and stimulating by the discriminating drinker:

Booth's Handbook of Cocktails and Mixed Drinks — John Doxat
Complete World Bartender Guide — Bob Sennett
The Fine Art of Mixing Drinks — David Embury
Grossman's Guide to Wines, Beers and Spirits — H. Lembeck
Michael Jackson's Pocket Bar Book
On Drink — Kingsley Amis
The Savoy Cocktail Book
Spirits, Aperitifs and Liqueurs — S.M. Tritton
Spirits and Liqueurs — Peter Hallgarten
Stirred not Shaken: the Dry Martini — John Doxat
Trader Vic's Bartender's Guide — Victor Bergeron

INDEX

INDEX

INDEX

INDEX

INDEX

INDEX

INDEX